Pages from My Life

A Liberal Arts Background for a Fundraising Career

Joseph Rappaport

Hamilton Books
A member of
The Rowman & Littlefield Publishing Group
Lanham • Boulder • New York • Toronto • Plymouth, UK

Contents

Preface

This book underscores career opportunities for service as a development officer for voluntary organizations. The text is based on my long experience in drafting and submitting proposals for support by foundations, government, and major corporations.

The text includes extensive excerpts from my funding proposals, as well as autobiographical information and a review of my educational background, including a Ph.D. degree, for a reader's self-comparison. The study is particularly relevant for young people who do not have graduate school training in specific professions such as law and finance. The text emphasizes how a general liberal arts background can serve as a basis for a successful career working with voluntary organizations that require grants to be obtained through the submission of fundraising proposals. The field also offers opportunities for individuals who have recently lost positions in the current economic recession.

The ability to draft funding proposals, as well as subsequent evidence of grants that were obtained, opened doors to a wide range of employment opportunities in the nonprofit sector.

I extend my loving thanks to my daughter Joyce Rappaport for her expert editorial work on my text. And I convey my loving appreciation to my daughter Ruth Rappaport for her typing of the chapters from my hand-draft.

Chapter One

The Early Years

I was born in the 1920s and spent my first years on Fox Street and Mohegan Avenue in the East Bronx, New York. Before the stock market crash in 1929, these were prosperous times for America. Yet my parents were quite poor, sustained by my father's work as a sewing machine repairman in the Manhattan garment district. He was trained by the ORT School (Organization for Rehabilitation Through Training). My father had a small office in the back of an electrical store on Sixth Avenue and 21st Street, owned by Benjamin Peters, whose secretary took calls seeking my father's repair services.

My father, Aaron B. Rappaport, and mother, Malka Lee, were Yiddish writers. His first book, *Through Walls of Fire* (1925), contains poems describing his experiences as an American soldier in France in 1918. My mother's first book, *Poems,* was published in Yiddish in 1932.

One of my earliest recollections, at the age of four, was entering the courtyard of a fifteen-unit housing collective, known as the Sholem Aleichem Houses, financed by shareholders in the northwest Bronx, joined by my parents. We had a two-bedroom apartment in the complex, dedicated primarily to the preservation of Yiddish cultural values.

MY PARENTS

The Sholem Aleichem Houses included Yiddish-speaking residents affiliated with the Workmen's Circle, dedicated to the shaping of a nicer, better world; other families clung to the ideal of state-owned factories and shops; and non-ideological residents were represented by the Unser Club, described as "card players" by the majority of residents. Most of the families sent their kids to two afternoon Yiddish schools organized by the Workmen's Circle and the

International Worker's Order. The respective teachers at these schools were Abraham Bromberg and Itche Goldberg.

Neither school accomplished a common goal of achieving a Yiddish-speaking new generation of children of immigrants from Central and Eastern Europe. Most of the kids in households in the complex could understand the spoken language of their parents. Yet very few of the afternoon school attendees could speak a fluent Yiddish in their adolescence and later years. This was the heritage of assimilation in America, despite the publication of four continuing Yiddish dailies in New York from 1900 to the 1950s. All the readers were immigrants from Europe. Tragically, the Nazi Holocaust in the World War II years ended the mass Jewish immigration into the United States. Other European survivors who made their way to Israel had to adapt to a Hebrew-speaking society.

As Yiddish writers, my parents lived through the years of the flowering of their language in our country into the 1970s. My father's second book, *Stories of the Shop* (1935), included tales and poems about the garment industry.

> Streets, buildings, windows
> From each window a song
> Metal energies do not tire
> The machines sing
> A metallic song

After his death in 1964, his Yiddish play, *Deborah the Prophetess,* was published in Israel.

My father always appeared to me to be quite frustrated by a life of physical labor, offset by strained efforts at literary expression. His father had settled on a dairy farm below Kingston, New York, and drew most of his income from a rooming house he built for summer guests. He donated some eight acres to my father, who in 1937 began construction of a series of bungalows, which ultimately comprised sixteen units in a beautiful setting for summer occupancy. This entailed further hard labor for my father, who personally installed all the electrical wiring and performed all the maintenance work. This left little time for his literary efforts, and his frustration was vented against his wife and two children. My sister Yvette was born in 1937.

At the same time, my father was well respected by non-Jewish neighbors who lived in surrounding upstate communities. The bungalows required plumbing installations by the Terwilliger Brothers, and work by local carpenters. His wartime service in the army in 1918 also brought him high regard. The local mailman, who made deliveries by car, always referred to his fellow veteran as Archie.

My father frequently commented about his experience on a troop vessel that was torpedoed in the English Channel. He assisted in hauling survivors over the side of the transport by rope onto lifeboats below. One of the soldiers bumped against my father's knee as he was being lowered from the sinking ship, and left my father with a life-long limp. He did not report his injury, he said, because he did not want his mother to be informed and left to worry.

My mother, known by her pen name Malka Lee, derived from her family name Leopold, came out of a town in the eastern part of the Austro-Hungarian empire in the Carpathian Mountains, called Monastrikh. Born in 1904, she grew up in an Orthodox family, which fled to Vienna during the First World War. Returning home, she began writing poetry in the German language, much to the consternation of her religious father, who believed that Jewish young ladies should be pursuing a marital life and not poesy. He stuffed her writings into the stovepipe over the kitchen oven.

When a ship ticket arrived from an aunt in America, intended for the father's emigration, Malka's mother insisted that the young poetess should leave instead. There would be no burning of poems in America. The decision ultimately led to the destruction of the family in the Holocaust, except for one brother who served in the Soviet army in World War II.

Malka arrived in the United States in 1921, promptly joined Jewish literary circles, and turned to the writing of poetry in Yiddish. She met Aaron Rappaport, and they married in 1922 in the dining hall of the rooming house built by Aaron's father on the upstate farm.

Malka Lee wrote a succession of books of poetry and prose after 1932, including *Gezangen* (1940), *Kinos fun Undzer Tsayt* (1945), *Durkh Loytere Kvaln* (1950), *Durkh Kindershe Oygn* (1955), *In Licht fun Doyres* (1961), *Untern Nusnboym* (1969), and *Mayselekh for Yoselen* (1969). The themes dealt with the Holocaust and the loss of her family. She died in 1976.

Her works had wide folk appeal, and she made many appearances before large audiences and reading circles. One gathering was visited by Maurice Schwartz, head of the classical Yiddish Art Theatre.

This acclaim had an impact on my parents' marriage, and although my father did not seek a separation or divorce, he was offset by her notoriety. The irony was that Yiddish literary critics and reviewers considered my father's writings to be superior.

My memories of childhood are also sharply focused on my grandfather. Daily, from the farm, he would drive his horse and buggy to the local creamery at the railroad station in Kyserike, New York with two large cans of milk. I would sit next to him on the wagon, and he would always be uttering his ritual prayers in Hebrew, while I looked up to him respectfully. On the Jewish High

Holy Days, farmers gathered in his house for services to read from his Torah scroll.

Another childhood experience on the farm was the birth of a calf, and our happy response as we stroked the newborn fondly. The next day, in the barn where winter's hay was being stored, I was shocked to see the calf hanging from a beam, stripped of its skin, ready to be cut up for eating.

SHOLEM ALEICHEM HOUSES

Summer's end would bring us back to our residence in the cooperative houses. The Sholem Aleichem Houses were established as a cooperative on Giles Place and Sedgwick Avenue in the Bronx in 1926 by Yiddish-speaking families. This was one of four similar Bronx cooperatives, including the Amalgamated Houses bordering on Van Cortlandt Park, and in the East Bronx, the left-wing Coops on Allerton Avenue and the Farband Houses, sponsored by a Labor Zionist organization.

The Sholem Aleichem Houses were built around a central courtyard, with gardens, over a maze of cellars containing a kindergarten and two classrooms, meeting rooms, a library, an auditorium, and cafeteria. Residents bought shares in the coop at $250 per room, but lacked trade union support, such as the nearby Amalgamated Houses established by the Amalgamated Clothing and Textile Workers.

The stock market crash in 1929 led to extensive unemployment among the residents, and the Sholem Aleichem Houses went into foreclosure the following year. The original investors lost their equities, and became renters of their apartments, now managed by a private landlord. My parents' apartment also accommodated a boarder.

On the other hand, the Depression of the 1930s heightened the radical idealism of the residents. They marched on Fifth Avenue in Manhattan on the Worker's Holiday, May 1. Neighbors shouted "Free the Scottsboro Boys" in protest against the conviction in 1931 of nine black teenagers for the alleged rape of two white girls in a freight car in Scottsboro, Alabama. In 1935, the United States Supreme Court ruled that the defendants' constitutional rights had been violated because blacks were excluded from jury rolls. The last of the imprisoned Scottsboro Boys was released in 1950.

At the Sholem Aleichem Houses, when the landlord attempted to evict tenants unable to pay their rents, collections were received from neighbors to cover their obligations. At times, furniture was removed by the landlord from apartments of nonpaying residents, and promptly brought back by neighbors.

The sense of collectivism, rooted in limited incomes and nurtured by radical ideology, is reflected in other patterns in my family's life. In the summer time, we would join others at my grandfather's upstate rooming house. Cooking in the joint dining hall was done by mothers who each had a small gas stove in a long row. Each family had a small table where meals were served in the shared dining section. The eighteen-room living quarters had only three bathrooms, shared by all the occupants. The rationale for this sacrifice of privacy was to escape the summertime heat in the city, in the absence of air conditioning, and the sense that children would be safeguarded from polio in the fresh air of a rural environment.

In the spirit of collectivism, residents participated in garment industry strikes. I recall strikers gathered in front of the Sholem Aleichem buildings demonstrating against a garment industry shop owner by the name of Mr. Lieber, who had an apartment in the complex. At one point, residents conducted a rent strike, and succeeded in lowering their monthly payments.

One of the ironies of the Depression was the leadership of pro-Soviet radicals in the labor movement. While dedicated ideologically to the overthrow of capitalism, these militants had a leading role in the ending of major abuses in the system. Through strikes and support of social legislation, the radicals led the fight for an eight-hour work day, a minimum wage, the end of child labor, and the elimination of sweat shops in the garment industry. While vilified by yellow journalism and accused of un-American activities, the immigrant radicals were instrumental in the shaping of a better society in towns and villages throughout the American heartland.

ELEMENTARY SCHOOL YEARS

Childhood memories, at random, include my recall of helping my grandfather gather hay from his fields to be stored in the barn to feed the milk cows through the winter. One summer day, two older grandchildren who lived in a nearby town, High Falls, helped deliver the hay wagon to the barn. The wagon tipped over and one of them, Morris May, was trapped under the fallen hay until rescued by neighbors with pitchforks.

Another time on my grandfather's farm, I fell off an apple tree and broke my arm. A tenant in the rooming house drove me to a doctor in Kingston, who put the arm in a cast, which was promptly signed by many friends. At the time, I was ten years of age.

A good memory at that age was watching the daily rehearsals for an elementary school play. On the day of the performance the leading actor called in sick (or had stage fright). I volunteered to take his place and did quite well as his stand-in. For the first time I witnessed the amazement and appreciation of a group of Irish school teachers at the capacity of a "smart Jewish kid." Only a few years earlier, my sole language at home had been Yiddish.

Another elementary school memory was my fascination with a 12:00 P.M. radio news broadcast by Gabriel Heatter. That was the hour when we were dismissed to go for lunch at our nearby apartments. To be able to listen to the start of the broadcast, I made up an excuse about a dietary need, and was permitted to run home five minutes ahead of my classmates. This interest in current events and world affairs was later reflected in my graduate studies in history.

A certain proclivity for going beyond the norm is characteristic of immigrant families seeking to adapt to a new environment. To deal with growing nearsightedness in my right eye, my mother took me to an optometrist at Columbia Presbyterian Hospital. When he prescribed eyeglasses, my mother reacted by asking if I could be fitted for a monocle (one glass). That was the era before contact lenses.

Also in my memory of childhood years was our use of rubber-banded bean shooters to hurl stones at birds. We missed all of the time, until one day we struck a bird sitting on the branch of a tree. We were aghast as we picked up the bird's body, cognizant that we had destroyed a living thing.

Another memory of elementary school was playing a violin with Bess Myerson, the future Miss America, also with a violin, at the graduation procession at P.S. 95. I had taken violin lessons for two years in a failing effort to cope with the instrument.

HIGH SCHOOL YEARS

I started middle school in the fall of 1937–with no Bar Mitzvah–attending De Witt Clinton High School within walking distance from my home. To get to the school, each morning I would walk through Fort Independence Park, across the street from my home, adjacent to the Jerome Park Reservoir, then to Mosholu Parkway, where the large school was located. This was an all-boys institution with high academic standards, whose principal was the rather austere A. Mortimer Clark.

My classmates included the future novelist James A. Baldwin, who served on the editorial board of *Magpie*, the school's literary journal. I brought a poem to James, about toys coming alive after midnight, which he quite promptly rejected with certain embarrassment. He later wrote a well-received volume, *Notes of a Native Son*, after leaving the United States and settling in France, where he was a prominent gay black resident and civil rights leader. Another classmate was Charles E. Silberman, author of a volume on crisis in

American schools, another study of black-white relations, as well as a volume on American Jewry.

My high school studies were productive, though I had poor grades in mathematics and chemistry, which put me on a path to a doctorate in American history. In my high school yearbook, published in 1941, I noted that I wanted to be a doctor. I had in mind a medical doctor, a destiny which did not come to pass.

My Yiddish-speaking background was demonstrated in a German-language class in high school. The teacher had us read a poem titled "Tannenbaum" (Christmas Tree), which included the line, "How green are your leaves." The instructor asked the class what was wrong with the description. I was the only one who answered, pointing out from my knowledge of the Yiddish term for "leaf," that Christmas trees do not bear leaves.

Classmates frequently attended football games in the Randall's Island Stadium, where the Clinton team opposed other high school players. We looked upon our helmeted players with certain awe, and I recall attending a class with a leading player, Bill Tracy. I was quite bewildered when he spoke to me directly, without condescension, as I responded haltingly. Thus are moulded heroes and their admirers.

I pause to note here that I had sustained an injury to my left knee several years earlier in a sandlot football game, an event that subsequently altered my life.

Politically, in the late 30s, in our housing complex, neighbors reacted sharply to the Spanish Civil War. There was active support for the Popular Front in its conflict with the Fascists led by General Francisco Franco. Following the 1936 victory at the polls by pro-Democratic candidates the government was attacked by Franco's nationalists and the Foreign Legion. This, in turn, prompted the Soviet dictator, Joseph Stalin, to dispatch pilots and political advisors in an effort to control the Popular Front. Promptly, Hitler and Mussolini sent arms and soldiers in support of the Fascist forces.

In the Sholem Aleichem Houses, several young men joined the Abraham Lincoln Brigade to help defend their radical brothers in Spain. All this was prelude to the world-wide conflict that broke out in 1939.

My recollections are of meetings in the auditorium of the complex, with calls for funds for the Lincoln Brigade. There were protests against the 1937 Neutrality Act, signed by President Roosevelt. Neighbors reacted in frustration as four Fascist columns converged in Madrid, supported by a fifth column inside the city. Failing in his efforts to control the Popular Front, Stalin withdrew armed Soviet support. By 1939, Franco ruled over Spain and gained United States recognition. All this had little impact on me, as I was engrossed in my high school studies and disdained left-wing politics.

Despite my poor grades in mathematics and chemistry, I qualified for admission at City College in the fall of 1941. This was the Princeton for the proletariat.

Then on December 7, 1941, Japanese aircraft struck Pearl Harbor, and Nippon forces seized Midway, Wake, and Guam. In his war message, President Roosevelt declared, "When we resort to force, as we now must, we are determined that this force shall be directed toward ultimate good, as well as against immediate evil." My college studies would soon be interrupted.

I well remember the day "that will live in infamy." My cousin, Ronald Levine, and I were listening to a radio broadcast to a New York Giants football game in the apartment of our friend, David Grubman, in the Sholem Aleichem Houses. At once, a voice came from the radio: "We interrupt this broadcast to announce that Japanese aircraft have bombed Pearl Harbor in Hawaii." Our lives were to proceed in new directions.

The following are further glimpses of my past during my high school years.

A striking memory relates to my seeking space to do my homework in a household where two parents needed desks for their own creative efforts. For a time I occupied my father's desk until he abruptly threw my school books and notes on the floor. I was relegated to a desk in the room where my young sister was sleeping. This arrangement continued for many months until the family moved to a larger apartment in the housing complex.

My first attraction to a young girl was at the age of fifteen. Violet Newman lived in the Sholem Aleichem Houses, and her parents rented a room for the summer in my grandfather's rooming house. She had joined us jumping from a rafter in the barn down to the hay below, and broke her arm. I shall forever remember her sweet face and quiet charm, as the first girl I ever kissed with affection. This was when she left the rooming house at the end of the summer. After her car departed, my mother slapped me in my face.

Characteristic of young men approaching manhood in their high school years was the bestowal of nicknames. While I remained Yossi, others were named for their proclivities. Two cardplayers were referred to as The Crooked Dollar and Ace. Another combed his hair in a certain style, and was accordingly called Duck. Mysteriously, "Hyogi" was the name attached to another young man who was killed in an airplane crash after the war.

Once a year, as young men, we would take the Yonkers Ferry to Fort Lee at the bottom of the New Jersey Palisades, and make our way to the top. My mother was fearful of this trek and tried to stop my joining the group. Another mother was able to dissuade her.

One haunting memory of my high school years was a young lady's call asking if I would escort her to her high school prom. I agreed. Then, lacking money for a floral piece, at the last moment I canceled this arrangement. To this day I have never forgiven myself for this crude behavior and the tearful night that I brought to the girl, never to be forgotten over our lifetimes.

COLLEGE YEARS

My attendance at City College continued through the spring of 1942, as work also proceeded in the building of my father's bungalow colony. I spent the summer digging drainage ditches for septic tanks adjacent to each bungalow. In the fall water had to be drained from all the pipes under each cabin to prevent the bursting of the pipes by frozen water.

The resort was soon called Lee-Ra Colony, named for my parents. Occupants then and later were Yiddish writers, including the playwright Leon Kobrin, the essayist B. J. Bialostotzky, the poet Michel Licht, the novelist Yankev Glatstein, and Avram Liessin, editor of the *Tsunkunft*. Most were European-born, now largely forgotten by new generations of American Jews. Their volumes are preserved by the Jewish Scientific Institute (YIVO) in New York. I recall the literary soirees on the lawns and in the social hall, known as the casino, where the writers exchanged views and critiques.

In the summer of 1942, in response to the drafting of men into the armed forces, a group of us went by train to the nearby town of Ellenville to register as prospective soldiers. World War II was now directly impacting on our young lives. My call to service came in the spring of 1943. My distraught mother rushed to the dean of the college to vainly seek a draft deferment. I then registered at a school in Manhattan for instruction in the Morse Code. Soon it was my turn to go for army examination at the Manhattan Center building.

The football injury to my left knee had over the years apparently healed, and I had quite forgotten about it. I did not refer to it during my draft examination, and was found to be fit for service. I received my recruitment notice in May 1943, and requested service in the Signal Corp as a forward artillery observer. This would involve reporting back to the artillery as a keypunch operator using the Morse Code.

On a day in May, my parents escorted me to Penn Station for the train to Fort Dix in New Jersey, to which regional draftees were assigned. It was a tearful departure on the first day that I had ever left home. No doubt, this conjured up memories in my father of leaving for army service in World War I. My mother had spoken earlier of her departure from her town in Poland en route to America. Her parents ran after the train as it left the station, never to be seen again.

At Fort Dix, a large group of draftees were addressed by a sergeant, who declared with a Polish accent: "You no soldier, you s- - t." We were assigned to barracks, and I shared a two-level bunk with an older, married recruit from Buffalo, who lamented his departure from his wife. The next day we were fitted with uniforms, and I looked at myself in the mirror with certain bravado. The uniform still remains in my closet.

There was no privacy in the bathrooms, where I observed a soldier on the regular staff of the camp, washing his genitals after apparent intercourse with a female in the nearby town. Manhood was thrust upon me in my initial contacts with the soldiers around me. After several days of marching, I was shipped to Fort Monmouth, a Signal Corp camp on the New Jersey coast. Within the complex, I was assigned to Camp Wood to start my basic training, consisting of lengthy marches, creeping under barbed wire, and jumping over wooden barricades. For the first time, I experienced sharp pain in my left knee.

So as I limped through various physical activities, I was subject to scrutiny by corporals and sergeants. A Jewish sergeant was particularly interested in determining whether my limp was legitimate. After an all-night stay in a forest, I was dispatched to the base hospital for comprehensive examination. I was also assigned to the kitchen to clean dishes. One afternoon, I was visited by my mother, who was kept waiting for several hours as I completed my tasks in the dining section.

One morning, I appeared before a panel of doctors and interns, who recommended my release. I left the hospital on August 12, 1943, with an honorable discharge, destined to spend my life with a stricken knee. Many years later, I stumbled on a sidewalk grating and broke my kneecap. In any event, I was entitled to all the benefits of the G. I. Bill of Rights, instituted in 1944, which included a range of educational benefits.

Thus, in the summer of 1943, I returned to the Lee-Ra bungalow colony, proudly wearing my uniform, which I did not shed until I started City College again in the fall. With the Bill of Rights, I transferred to New York University to complete my baccalaureate studies. I encountered the ire of a history professor, Ralph Flanders, who was an outright racist, and asked me if I wanted to fight, and applied for admission to the Columbia University Graduate School as a major in American history. Thus, in the fall of 1944, the "kid from The Bronx" entered a new phase in his life.

In passing, my life turned out different than the lives of the two boys with whom I sat listening to the announcement of the Japanese attack on Pearl Harbor. David Grubman was sent by the U.S. Army to medical school and became a doctor. Ronald Levine was to become an Air Force Warrant Officer. In contrast, my army service ended during basic training. We anticipated none of this as we listened to accounts of the Japanese assault.

Chapter Two

Graduate School

My graduate studies marked the beginning of my capacity as a fund-raising proposal writer and development officer for nonprofit organizations. This was a career that continued for over fifty years, and serves as an example for students in social studies as ways in which they can look to voluntary organizations that continually seek development officers to develop support from foundations and government.

At Columbia, starting in 1944, I attended classes and seminars conducted by John A. Kraut, Henry S. Commager, Harry Carmen, and Allan Nevins, professors of history in the Fayerweather Building on Columbia's compact Morningside Heights campus. My interest remained in American Jewish history, which I thought even then was an integral part of American history as a discipline. My initial goal was to obtain a position as an instructor in an American university.

As a major in American history, I rather naively embarked on a Master's thesis on the Russian backgrounds of Jewish immigrants into the United States. There was no one in the American history faculty who was qualified to guide me. For apparent fear of being accused of antisemitism, no faculty member would advise me, at the time, that the history of Jews in the United States was rejected by academia as being an integral part of the American story. Nor was I advised that my job prospects were infinitesimal in college academia. The situation has entirely changed, and I may have helped bring this about.

Meanwhile, armed conflict continued throughout the world in 1944–45 amidst a Holocaust taking place in Europe aimed at the destruction of the Jewish people. As I worked in my cubicle in the Columbia library, Germany was defeated in May 1945, and American soldiers stormed the beaches of Pacific islands held by the Japanese. My Master's thesis was beginning to emerge, to be titled "Russian Jewry: A Study of Immigrant Backgrounds." My degree was conferred in 1947, and I was later accepted as a Ph.D. candidate.

There were profound developments taking place in the world, which I could now follow as a veteran of the United States Army. In February and March 1945, American armed forces seized the volcanic island of Iwo Jima, marked by the raising of our flag atop Mount Suribachi, as photographed by Joe Rosenthal. America was now ready to strike at the Japanese mainland, with the prospect of the loss of over a million soldiers. Then, in August, the city of Hiroshima was destroyed by an atomic bomb. On August 15, the Japanese emperor Hirohito announced his country's surrender. Times Square in Manhattan was gripped by joyous fervor.

During all these momentous developments, I continued quietly to research my master's thesis. Only in the long term, as a proposal writer, would there be any concrete significance in the research and writing effort.

MASTER'S THESIS

My introduction to the thesis underscores the political oppression of the Russian Jews, and notes that I was attempting "to define the effects of Tsarist disabilities upon the economic life of the Jehovites" (as I called them). The preface notes that I would trace the pogroms, occupational patterns, and structure of Jewish communal life. In retrospect, the text demonstrates a certain flair for writing, which I would later also develop in my efforts at screenwriting.

The first chapter of the thesis covers the classic age of Jewish communal development up to the seventeenth century in Poland under Tsarist rule. "The leeches that clung to the lining of the cloak of materialism which a small portion of Jewry had thrown over its shoulders began to drain the rich blood from the spiritual body." At the same time, the Jews served as scapegoats for the evils in Russia's economy, societal structure, and governance upon which Tsarist rule rested. The Jews were relegated to a Pale of Settlement and urban ghettoes from which an emigration began. The pogroms that followed the assassination of Tsar Alexander II on March 13, 1881, led to a surge of departure from the land.

My research included volumes by Salo W. Baron, I. Friedlander, S. W. Dubnow, I. M. Rubinov, and the co-authors M. L. Margolis and A. Marx. Of special relevance were manuscript autobiographies written in 1943–1944 in a contest dealing with Jewish life in Eastern Europe, sponsored by the Jewish Scientific Institute (YIVO).

The second chapter of my Master's thesis delves into the economic condition of Russia's five million Jews, centered in poverty-stricken Lithuania and White Russia during the transition from feudalism to capitalism. I wrote: "Whereas 37 percent of the gainfully occupied Jews poured their sweat into skilled mechanical and manufacturing tasks, only 15 percent of the working Slavs were so employed." More than one-third of economically active Jews pursued trade and commerce. Economic disruptions in the shaping of a capitalist society had a heavy effect on Jewish artisans, leading to a mass exodus. Many had pursued livelihoods, I noted, in the production and marketing of clothing, which helped them to blend into New York's garment industry.

I summarized the root causes of Jewish mass departure in the following observation: "Overpopulation, occupational disproportion, and religio-political oppression in an unbalanced, poverty-stricken economy, further strained by the growth of an unbenevolent industrial-Capitalism."

In retrospect, another observation from my Master's thesis appears to point the way to a writing style that marked my efforts over many years as a successful fundraiser based on the preparation of proposals: "Finally, the reverberations of the hammering machine, powered by the Capitalist entrepreneur, was slowly shattering the rotted foundation upon which the artisan's bench rested."

In my thesis narrative, I emphasize that the increase in machine production reduced the need for manual laborers, who looked to emigration as an inescapable means of earning a livelihood. At the same time, Jewish merchants and traders were affected by the growing poverty of the masses. This extended to Jewish dealers in farm goods, hit by falling sales, the expansion of the railroads, and discriminatory laws and practices.

In the third and final chapter of my thesis, I dealt with the impact of an emerging capitalism on the religious roots of the Jewish community. Sectarian beliefs saw Jews clinging to ancient and medieval traditions, resisting contemporary pressures. Each community had a synagogue, burial society, cemetery, and provisions for kosher food. Confronting antisemitism, the Jewish community isolated itself from non-Jewish neighbors and practices. Russian Jews chose the path of martyrdom in the face of Slavic intolerance.

And yet there was an economic dependence upon the broad society that surrounded the Jewish community. This was exemplified by weekly gatherings in market squares where products were exchanged with non-Jewish neighbors. I wrote: ". . . the weakening of agrarian stability, the death throes of the handicraft economy, and the growth of the Capitalist system shook the Jewish community to its foundations. Its relative economic independence was destroyed, and the waters of the economic sea swept over it."

The religious community was also increasingly challenged by a growing worldliness, modernity, and progressivism. The rabbinate and councils of elders were challenged by secularism, Zionism, and socialism. Ruling authorities within the Jewish community no longer had free rein over the preparation of census lists, the certification of tradesmen, and the assessment and collection of state and communal taxes. The abolition of the councils of elders by imperial decree in 1844 further disrupted Jewish patterns and opened the way to emigration as a means of escaping internal upheavals. Charitable, educational, and occupational organizations facilitated the exodus. I wrote: "The blood stream of Judaism had flowed for many centuries; no constricting legal tourniquets could halt the pulsations of its spiritual arteries."

The formation of the Jewish Labor Bund in 1897 in Lithuania marked the growing separation of Jewish labor from communal controls. The emergence of a Jewish factory proletariat was marked by a growing emigration from the village workers guild to the Jewish labor movement in America.

In the final short chapter of my thesis, I summarized my research on emigration described in the manuscript autobiographies sponsored in 1943–1944 by the Jewish Scientific Institute (YIVO), as well as published autobiographies written by immigrants from Russia.

A basic pattern in the migration was the presence of family members in the United States, who sent ship tickets to the majority of the immigrants. I noted this in the case of my mother's departure from Poland. Thus, paid passage to the Land of Liberty was a way out of Russian poverty and antisemitism.

I concluded my thesis with the following words:

> Immigrants are dreamers. They are dissatisfied human beings. They pursue illusions molded largely by poverty. America became synonymous with every vision and every hopeful fancy. When the Jew heard the call of the Pied Piper of the New World, the dance of the dreamers commenced, and a million-folk listened to the splash of ocean waters.

In early 1947, I continued my studies in American history at Columbia University. With ongoing course attendance under the G. I. Bill, I soon was forced to choose a topic for my doctoral dissertation. In view of my upbringing and academic background, I was oriented to the American Jewish field, with little consideration of prospects at the time for a career in college teaching.

I felt encouraged at this point by the offer of an instructorship in an evening course in European history at Brooklyn College. This entailed a one-hour subway trip from my parents' home in the northwest Bronx to Flatbush Avenue beyond the middle of Brooklyn. I promptly accepted the position, which meant teaching a class of largely older students. The lengthy trip meant that I could also prepare for my lectures on the subway. At the same time, the daytime hours could be scheduled for my course attendance at Columbia. My teaching also offered the opportunity to offer European history as a minor, with American history, in my doctoral studies at Columbia.

The fates proved to be kind to me, as I believe that my discussion of European history in my doctoral oral examination in 1949 was superior to my responses to questions about American history. I have always advocated teaching as a means of qualifying for advanced doctoral studies.

My teaching experience at Brooklyn College, which continued for a year, left me with a number of marked impressions. Namely, I was not a highly qualified instructor. My delivery was repetitive, and I was not sufficiently domineering. My students did well in their final exams, but I was left with the sense that a lifetime to be spent teaching the same subject matter over and over each year would not be personally fulfilling.

Brooklyn College, under long-time president Harry D. Gideonse, was also the scene of the dismissal of a number of left-wing faculty members. Dr. Gideonse defended the House Un-American Activities Committee, and criticized Zionist leaders for seeking Jewish emigration to the newly created state of Israel. Gideonse later went on to head the Washington-based research organization, Freedom House, and then was chancellor of the New School for Social Research in New York City.

I personally wanted to be out of Brooklyn College, and submitted my resignation to Dr. Jesse Clarkson, chairman of the history department. He reacted negatively when I remarked that I believed that the older evening-session students were on a par with daytime enrollees. He accepted my resignation.

Nineteen forty-eight was a good year. In January, I was introduced at Columbia University to Naomi Chaitman from Montreal. It was a good match. She was a student in the anthropology department, working with Margaret Mead and Ruth Benedict on a project sponsored by the United States Office of Naval Research, involving the study of foreign cultures at a distance. As a prototype, the project selected the East European Jewish community for analysis, looking to the application of methodologies developed in the study of other overseas groups. This would have relevance for American armed forces moving into unfamiliar areas.

In the introduction to the resulting volume, written by Mark Zborowski and Elizabeth Herzog, titled *Life Is with People* (1952), Margaret Mead wrote: "Naomi Chaitman, in addition to her outstanding skill as an interviewer, brought her anthropological training and a living experience with Eastern European Jewish culture, gained in the learned environment of her parents' home and through wide contacts with the Jewish community in Montreal and in New York." The study was directly in line with my own master's thesis on Russian Jewry.

Naomi was a tall, beautiful woman, born in 1926, and we were immediately attracted to each other. Besides, I was something of a "catch" in her circles as the son of two well-known Yiddish writers. Quite soon, I visited her parents' home in Montreal, where her father was principal of an elementary day school that emphasized the Yiddish language and culture. This was a city sharply divided by its French-speaking population, the Anglos, and immigrant Jews. All of Naomi's family and friends were fluent in Yiddish, including the doctor who delivered her at birth, Solomon Gold, who himself had earlier been a teacher in the Jewish day school.

It wasn't long before Naomi and I were engaged, and we were married in June 1948, in a restaurant on the lower Second Avenue in New York. The union took place here–not in Montreal–because there were bungalows to be rented at Lee-Ra Colony. After a short honeymoon in Schroon Lake, the married couple promptly moved into a small apartment on Sedgwick Avenue in the Bronx, in a building owned by a relative in my father's family.

The book that Naomi helped prepare on the Jewish community was well-received by anthropologists as a prototype for the study of folkways at a distance. Yet, at a forum of Jewish scholars, it was strongly criticized for its analysis of village customs. Mark Zborowski angrily stomped out of the session.

There was a darker side to Zborowski, which emerged following the publication of the volume. He allegedly had started as a Soviet agent in Paris in the early 1930s, spying on Western followers of Leon Trotsky, who had been ousted by the Russian Bolsheviks. Zborowski was implicated in the theft of Trotsky's archives from an historical institute in Paris. Zborowski came to the United States in 1940, and was later apprehended by the FBI for spying on the Trotskyites in New York. He served time in a federal prison for perjury in the prosecution of a Soviet spy team in New York, and died in 1990.

None of this is reflected in *Life Is with People,* which is a product of a joint effort by anthropologists headed by Margaret Mead. Dr. Mead was an eminent scholar and author of many volumes starting with *Coming of Age in Samoa* (1928). She served as curator of ethnology at the American Museum of Natural History from 1926 to 1969.

At this point, I was faced with the choice of a topic for my doctoral dissertation. I chose to survey immigrant Jewish reactions during World War I, based on a study of the Yiddish press. I undertook this effort even before taking an oral exam to formally qualify as a doctoral candidate.

I vividly recall Dr. Henry S. Commager sitting through my oral exam on American history reading a newspaper. Professor Allan Nevins advised me of my acceptance, with certain reservations, after I left the panel to await the final decision. Since then, I have always advised doctoral candidates to seek a teaching job to broaden their knowledge in a chosen field.

My wife was now prepared to help support a scholarly husband as he continued his research on immigrant Jewish war reactions. Naomi obtained a position as a teacher at an afternoon Yiddish school, maintained by the Workmen's Circle. In addition, she took on Yiddish translation assignments from individuals interested in the contents of family letters and papers.

Doctoral Dissertation

In my dissertation research, I reviewed reactions to unfolding events, starting in 1914, in six Yiddish dailies in the United States, as well as a range of weekly and monthly periodicals. Following the assassination, on June 28, of Archduke Francis Ferdinand, heir to the Hapsburg throne, the Yiddish press waffled between support of emerging alliances. When, finally, Germany faced Russia on the Eastern Front, Jewish immigrants overwhelmingly supported the cultured Germans in their confrontation with the Russian barbarians who had bathed in Jewish blood.

On October 2, 1914, the *California Yiddishe Shtimme* intoned, "Regardless of our great love for England and France we are forced to express the wish. . . that the defeat of the Allies be so great that Russia will be wiped off the earth. . . ." In New York, the daily *Varheit* suffered a sharp drop in circulation because of the pro-Ally position of its editor. Abraham Cahan, editor of the *Forverts,* the largest Yiddish daily, wrote on August 1st, "All civilized people sympathize with Germany, every victorious battle against Russia is a source of joy."

Through 1915, against the avalanche of Allied propaganda, immigrant American Jews attacked the hypocritical British alliance with Russia. "A German victory at Verdun," the Forverts declared on June 14, 1915, "will be a victory over Nicholas' pogromists" and a defense of the honor of Jewish women and innocent Jewish men. Henrietta Szold, founder of Hadassah, declared at the 1915 convention of the Zionist Federation: "I do not believe that the Allies are fighting in favor of the principle of smaller nationalities." Most Zionists continued to look to Turkey, which was in control of Palestine, for the establishment of the visionary national home for the Jews. Rabbi Stephen S. Wise looked to uninterrupted Jewish settlement in Palestine under continued Turkish rule. American Zionists had no clue that the 1916 secret

Sykes-Picot Agreement between England and France looked to British control over part of Palestine.

Meanwhile, Jewish organizations strongly supported the American embargo movement, which sought to ban the export of war materials. Jewish newspapers and periodicals published embargo appeals drafted by the American Association of Foreign Newspapers, and financed by the German Information Bureau. The Jewish Socialist Federation joined the United German Societies of New York City in sponsoring a peace and embargo gathering at Madison Square Garden on June 24, 1915, which led to the formation of the Friends of Peace organization. The October 1915 convention of the International Ladies Garment Workers Union went on record opposing the shipment of "life necessities" to Europe.

My dissertation traces Jewish reactions to German submarine attacks against vessels carrying materials to the Allies. The sinking of the giant British liner *Lusitania* off the Irish coast on May 7, 1915, marked the beginning of a schism in Jewish circles over outright support of the German war effort. Editors conceded that the vessel was carrying munitions, yet they could not overlook the loss of 128 Americans in the sinking. I wrote: "The marginal man–the Jewish immigrant–was now torn between the demands of American patriotism and private views of the best interests of East European brethren." The tide was beginning to shift for American immigrant Jewry.

In the face of the preparedness movement for the arming of America in the event that the nation would be forced to go to war, the Jewish community moved from a rabid pro-Germanism to a crusade for peaceful mediation to stop the war. This, it was hoped, would at least leave Poland under the control of the conquering Germans and maintain Turkish rule over Palestine. The Yiddish press hailed Henry Ford for financing the sailing of a peace ship in December 1915 with its cargo of intellectuals to get the soldiers out of the trenches by Christmas. As war continued, some socialists looked with favor at the Bolshevik Vladmir Lenin's call for revolutionary action to end the war. The more moderate editor of the *Forverts,* Abraham Cahan, supported the peace movement with the view that an armistice would allow Germany to retain its Eastern conquests.

In the presidential election in 1916, a majority of Jews supported Woodrow Wilson and the peace plank in his platform. He had also nominated Louis D. Brandeis for the Supreme Court early in 1916, and Brandeis was confirmed by the Senate in June. On November 2nd, Wilson attracted a crowd of 20,000 when he appeared at Cooper Union on the Lower East Side. Yiddish journals hailed his election as a demonstration for peace.

At this point, my doctoral dissertation paused to describe the growth of the Zionist movement in America, which had enduring impact extending to the present day. I noted that World War I stirred a survivalist impulse among all immigrants, including many Jews who looked to the establishment of a national home in the land of their ancient ancestors. America's wartime prosperity diminished the appeal of the class struggle ideals, which blended with the Zionist emphasis on diplomacy and chartism. Addressing the Eastern Council of Reform Rabbis in June 1915, Louis D. Brandeis declared: "Every American Jew who aids in advancing the Jewish settlement in Palestine. . . will likewise be a better man and a better American for doing so."

Brandeis saw in Zionism a means of securing for the world the full benefit of Jewish talent given the opportunity for unhampered development in a homeland. He described the aims of the movement to President Wilson, and sought to engage the interest of the French and British ambassadors. The activities of the Chaim Weizmann group in England gained the support of Brandeis's Provisional Executive Committee for General Zionist Affairs, organized in 1914. English Zionists urged the British conquest of Palestine in the war against Turkey, with free Jewish immigration and ultimate home rule. On December 14, 1914, Lord Arthur J. Balfour remarked to Weizmann: "I believe that when the guns stop firing you may get your Jerusalem."

Soon the British and French were negotiating the secret Sykes-Picot Agreement of 1916, assigning Palestine to Britain. On March 22, 1917, Balfour, now Foreign Secretary, advised Weizmann that a joint Anglo-American protectorate ought to be established in Palestine. Instead, Weizmann wrote to Brandeis that Britain should alone set up such a regime. The stage was being set for the Balfour Declaration on November 2, 1917, looking to the development in Palestine of a national home for the Jewish people under a British mandate. I devoted a full chapter in my dissertation to the Balfour Declaration.

Another chapter in my study is titled "America Goes to War." In December 1916, Britain rejected an invitation by the Imperial German government to enter into direct peace talks. The Yiddish press was furious that, in the words of the New York *Varheit,* "The Allies have tossed off the cloak of righteousness and martyrdom." The Allies' demand that the Germans evacuate all conquered territories was termed stupid and criminal by Yiddish newspaper editors. Leon Trotsky, who arrived in the United States in January 1917, wrote in the *Forverts,* under his original name, Leo Bronstein, that the prolongation of the conflict would allow the tsar to don the mantle of "spiritual leadership." Immigrant Jews hailed President Wilson's address on January 22, 1917, in the Senate, in which he called for "peace without victory."

But the die was cast when the German government announced the resumption of unrestricted submarine warfare. On February 3, 1917, Wilson informed Congress that he had severed diplomatic ties with Germany. Now the mettle of all immigrant Jews was being tested. On the left, Congressman Meyer London attacked war agitation by "lip patriots," and in the New York State Assembly, Abraham Shiplacoff called for a national referendum on the issue of entry into the conflict. Responding to Leon Trotsky's advocacy of resistance to war, the editor of the *Forverts* declared that the United States is a new fatherland for the Jews and urged that all thinking Americans "see to make this a better home."

The dilemma of American immigrant Jewry was resolved in March 1917 with the abdication of the Russian tsar, and the establishment of a provisional government soon to be headed by Alexander Kerensky. I wrote in my dissertation:

> Never was there a Socialist gathering quite like the one that took place in the old Madison Square Garden on March 20. Some 20,000 joyous celebrants shouted wildly and danced in the aisles as [speakers] . . . sang the glories of the democratic revolution in beloved "Matushka Rossiya" (Mother Russia). Following the gathering, the audience blended with the theatre crowd on Second Avenue and East Broadway, and long lines marched to Rutgers Square amidst cries of "Long live the Russian Revolution!"

For most immigrant Jews, the Allies had become the hope for universal Jewish emigration and the realization of Zionist goals. Now the war was more clearly for the preservation of democracy, and many Yiddish newspaper editors supported the Jewish League of American Patriots. On April 2nd, President Wilson called for a declaration of war. While radicals still voiced their reservations, the tide was overwhelmingly in favor of support for the new American homeland in its quest for the emancipation of humanity from the threat of German autocracy. On May 14th, 20,000 flocked to a war bond rally in Seward Park, New York, organized by the League of Jewish Patriots.

Socialist antiwar stirrings remained, exemplified by the Morris Hillquit campaign for the New York City mayoralty in the fall of 1917. He refused to accept "the native theory" that Germany's defeat would bring lasting peace. The Bolshevik Revolution in Russia further stirred ideological opposition to the war. Yet, my dissertation includes a chapter on the year 1918, which I described as the Year of the Messiah.

A remarkable spirit gripped American Jewry in the last months of hostilities. This was a time of great expectations, when out of the crucible of the conflict a "brave new world" was seen to be emerging. America's entry into the war "for democracy," the Balfour Declaration, and the ten days in Petrograd that shook the world each had meaning for diverse elements. Events seemed to hold out for Jews and all the proletariat the promise of emancipation from the oppression of the Diaspora and capitalism. The first step would be the defeat of Prussian military and commercial autocracy. Wilson's "Fourteen Points" address before Congress on January 8, 1918 underscored the principle of self-determination of peoples, which was welcomed by Jews as the promise of independence for Poland and Romania, the creation of a League of Nations, and support for Jewish statehood in Palestine.

Sidney Hillman and Joseph Schlossberg of the Amalgamated Clothing Workers Union wrote in March:

> . . . our hearts go out to heroic Russia; we are tempted to say holy Russia, martyred Russia. Russia's role in this frightful world tragedy gives the struggle against German militarism a new meaning, new substance.

The Jewish Socialist Federation at its national conference on May 10–12 supported this position. The convention of the ILGWU in May saw the war as a phase in the unfolding of a socialist world. At the same time, the non-radical Yiddish press saw Allied intervention in Russia, following the March signing of the Treaty of Brest-Litosvk by the Leninist regime and Germany, as a means of getting rid of the hated Bolsheviks.

As the war approached its finale, the American Jewish community was gripped by both a messianic religious fervor and socialist expectation of world revolution. Rabbi Stephen S. Wise, a former pacifist, now described the radicals as being of the "basement and cellar type," serving the interests of Germany. The Zionist spokesman Jacob De Haas characterized his movement: ". . . all who are against us can be said to be against America as well." The *Yiddishe Tageblatt* wrote on March 27th, "The battle for a Jewish state in Palestine is being fought in Flanders." On August 21, 1918, President Wilson formally endorsed the Balfour Declaration.

With the abdication of the German Kaiser, the World War came to an end on November 11th. Abraham Cahan, editor of the *Forverts,* rushed forth to embrace the world revolution. "The old is shattered—the ugly German throne! Socialists are at the helm! Hearts are full of joy, nerves dance with enthusiasm; there is so much happiness . . ."

Yet my dissertation ends with a quotation from the Yiddish *Chicago Courier* on Armistice Day. Amidst all the jubilation, the daily could only declare: "The crisis in Europe is beginning—and God only knows how it will end."

The completion of my doctoral dissertation was made possible by my dear wife's dedication and financial support of our household. Indeed, in 1950, she had become pregnant, and sought an abortion, which at the time was illegal in our state. She discussed this with older friends connected with

Columbia's anthropology department. An appointment was set up with a doctor in midtown Manhattan, who performed an illegal operation. Naomi's fright and guilt over the destruction of the fetus left an indelible mark. Ironically, we later moved to Manhattan very close to the abortionist's office, and frequently passed his door. The idealist pursuit of learning also left a legacy of painful regret for a child that was not permitted to be brought into the world.

Chapter Three

The Real World

ALLAN NEVINS

I was granted my Columbia University doctorate in June 1951. Professor Harry Carmen of the history department recommended me to the business school of City College, which led to a short-term teaching assignment. In the interim, my wife and I initiated a correspondence with numerous colleges across the nation seeking an instructorship. There had to be reference to my doctoral dissertation based on a study of the Yiddish press, and not a single invitation came back asking me for an interview.

In this effort, our friend Leila Bravmann assisted in the preparation of my inquiry. Leila and her husband, Edgar, a refugee from Germany, were active in the movement to train Americans for resettlement on collective farms in Israel.

Fortunately, Columbia history professor Allan Nevins soon offered me a research assistantship, starting in 1952. I spent several months at the National Archives in Washington studying the work of Montgomery C. Meigs, head of the United States Quartermaster Services during the Civil War years. I poured over copybooks that recorded the daily work of supplying arms and equipment for the expanding Union Army in 1861–1865.

The year 1952 was highlighted by the birth of our first child, Joyce. Bright and beautiful, she was destined to follow in her parents' footsteps as scholar and researcher, starting with her attendance at the specialized high school, The Bronx High School of Science. Unlike her father, Joyce did well in mathematics and chemistry, and went on to obtain a doctorate in English literature at York University (Toronto). Subsequently, she served as English professor at Chapman University in Sacramento, specializing in eighteenth-century English literature. She then served as copy chief for the two-volume *YIVO Encyclopedia of Jewish Literature in Eastern Europe.* Joyce presently is managing editor of the multivolume series on Jewish culture and civilization, sponsored by the Posen Foundation, being published by the Yale University Press.

Our second beautiful daughter, Ruth, was born in 1955. Gifted in music and song, she served as solo vocalist and guitarist with The Poodles, a female folk music ensemble performing throughout New England, New York, and Europe. After coordinating meetings of the International Physicians for the Prevention of Nuclear War, Ruth was appointed conference manager for the Education Development Center, based in Newton, Massachusetts. EDC is a leading educational organization, sponsoring international meetings of scholars and school administrators on vital academic issues. At the same time, Ruth is active in Watertown, Massachusetts, as a prominent volunteer in dealing with public issues, and continues to perform as a folk musician.

My research efforts for Professor Allan Nevins continued in connection with his preparation of the history of the Ford Motor Company. I had covered one episode in my doctoral dissertation–the sailing of the Peace Ship to Europe on December 4, 1915. With financing by Henry Ford, the initiative of the pacifist Rosika Schwimmer, and participation by Herman Bernstein, editor of the Yiddish daily *Tog,* the ship left for Norway. Henry Ford's initiative failed to sway the Allies and Germany, and left an embittered automaker who later criticized radical Jews for their initiative in this venture.

At this point in this memoir, I am providing a chronological listing of the range of my positions from 1954 to 2000. This includes a number of work assignments conducted jointly in the same years.

1954–1958   Research Director, American Jewish History Center, Jewish Theological Seminary of America (New York)

1958–1963   Assistant, Hon. Herbert H. Lehman, former New York governor and U.S. senator

1964–1966   Consultant, Office of Urban Studies, City University of New York
Senior Consultant, Office of Deputy Mayor
City Administrator, City of New York

Director, Special Studies, Temporary
Commission on City Finances, City of New York

1967–1970   Director, Research Department, Federation of Jewish Philanthropies of New York

1971–1974   Associate Director of Development, Fordham University

1972–1974   Consultant, State Charter Revision Commission for New York City
Consultant, State Study Commission for New York City

1974–1976   Consultant, Phoenix House (New York City)

1974–1976   Staff Consultant, Allergy Foundation of America (New York City)
Staff Consultant, Citizens Budget Commission (New York City)

1975   Consultant, Arthur Andersen & Company
Consultant, Economic Development Council of New York City
Consultant, Citizens Union Foundation (New York City)

1976–1977   Director of Development and College Relations, Utica College of Syracuse University

1978–1979   Senior Assistant, Deputy Mayor for Policy, City of New York

1979–1981   President, Dropsie University (Philadelphia)

1981–1985   Assistant to President, March of Dimes Birth Defects Foundation (White Plains, New York)

1986–1990   Independent Contractor, Personnel Placement

1990–1995   Senior Development Officer, Touro College (New York)

1995–2000   Independent Contractor, Personnel Placement

American Jewish History Center

In January 1954, I started as research director for the American Jewish History Center, established at the Jewish Theological Seminary, a rabbinical training institution in New York City. Sponsored by the clothier Louis M. Rabinowitz, my mentor Allan Nevins served as co-director of the center. Rabbi Moshe Davis, provost of the Seminary, served as joint director. The project undertook the preparation of the history of Jewish communities in Milwaukee, Los Angeles, Cleveland, Montreal, Vineland (New Jersey), and Miami Beach. My initial role was to research the origins of these Jewish communities as noted in national Jewish periodicals in the nineteenth century. My work on the Cleveland and Miami Beach communities are prototypes for the effort undertaken by the American Jewish History Center.

At the conference of the American Jewish History Center in Cleveland on December 1, 1955, convened by Western Reserve University and Rabbi Jack J. Herman of the Community Temple, I spoke on the relationship of Jewish and general residents in the development of a range of American communities. In line with my doctoral dissertation on Jewish reactions to events during World War I, my remarks reflected my interest in comparing Jews and Yankees in Cleveland.

When a survey party of the Connecticut Land Company, led by General Moses Cleveland, came to the confluence of the Cuyahoga River and Lake Erie in 1796, they brought with them an image of the pattern of a Connecticut town with place for a house of worship. The first Bavarian Jews to reach Cleveland formed the Israelitish Society in 1839, and soon had a Torah scroll and synagogue. I had noted this in my research in national Jewish periodicals, which included reports on the emerging Jewish community in Cleveland. The local newspaper also began printing items on Jewish residents.

When a new synagogue was dedicated on Eagle Street in August 1846, the editor of the *Cleveland Herald* noted the following inscription on the wall: "A Testimonial of Gratitude to J. M. Woolsey, Esq. and Lady for their liberal assistance in erecting this edifice."

In my remarks at the Cleveland conference in 1955, I commented:

> Striving actively, and very consciously, for adjustment, the Jewish community began to adopt features of the social organization of the general community. It initially turned to the Woolseys for assistance and to the Baptist congregation for the design of its house of worship. Early Jewish literary, fraternal, and welfare institutions were a synthesis–a cross fertilization–of European-Jewish features and established Cleveland forms.

In my closing comments, I noted that as the Jews of Cleveland developed their own community, their cultural organizations and business firms became an integral part of the life of the city. Thus, they helped to build the city.

As part of its series of communal studies, the American Jewish History Center in 1956 launched a study of South Florida Jewry. Rabbi Irving Lehman of Temple Emanu-el, Miami Beach, was regional coordinator for the project, which obtained support from the Greater Miami Jewish Federation.

The South Florida study had personal importance in relation to my subsequent work as an organizational fundraiser and government administrator. I made several trips to Miami and Miami Beach, visiting local institutions, observing their programs, and gaining a knowledge of their financial procedures. An initial brochure, published in 1956, *The Jewish Community of Miami Beach*, is summarized here. The authors were Rabbi Irving Lehmann and myself.

The preface notes that in 1918, Miami Beach was incorporated as a city notwithstanding a total of less than 100 registered voters. The founders had visions of a resort citadel rising from the tree-tangled sand bar. Forty years later, the island had over 50,000 permanent residents, and had become one of the fastest-growing Jewish communities in the nation.

The brochure traces the origins of Miami Beach going back to 1870, when Henry Lum set foot on the island with a vision of planting palm trees to grow coconuts. Lum was soon joined on nearby acreage by John S. Collins, who later helped turn coconuts into a resort colossus.

When Isador Cohen arrived in Miami from Savannah in 1896, there was only one dwelling in Miami Beach built by Charlie Lum. "'This is going to be a wonderful city,'" Cohen wrote in his diary describing Miami, "'Buildings are springing up in every direction as if by magic.'" Across the bay, John S. Collins had begun turning mangrove into building sites. By 1906, Miami Beach's first hotel was opened by Dick Smith. Six years later, John Collins and his son-in-law Thomas J. Pancoast undertook construction of a viaduct to the mainland, described as "'the longest wooden bridge in the world.'" By the mid-1920s, Miami Beach had 2,500 residents, with a number of Jewish-owned hotels and apartment houses on the lower part of the island.

The origins of Jewish communal life in the City of Miami date from the 1890s. The local daily, *The Metropolis*, noted on September 11, 1896: "The Jewish holiday commenced Monday night and has been generally observed by the Jewish people of Miami. The festivities lasted two days. A Jewish organization was perfected Monday with David Singer president and M. Bucholtz secretary and treasurer. The membership numbers 22." By 1912, the Jewish community in Miami had enough substance to form an ongoing congregation, with weekly services, later known as Beth David. In 1920, a new site at Northwest Third Avenue became the center of Jewish communal activity in Miami. A second congregation, Temple Israel, formed in 1922, later built an edifice on Northwest Nineteenth Street.

The 1920s saw the rapid expansion of Jewish communal activity in Miami, extending beyond a synagogal base, an array of philanthropic, social, and cultural organizations emerged. These included the Jewish Welfare Bureau, the Sholom Lodge of B'nai B'rith, Hadassah, a Workmen's Circle branch, a section of the National Council of Jewish Women, and a branch of the Zionist Organization of America. Two weekly periodicals also appeared. All of this had an impact on Jewish residents across the bay in Miami Beach.

Even as hotel façades spread along the beaches, culminating with over 300 resorts by 1941, Jewish communal life was also evolving in Miami Beach. The Beth Jacob congregation began services in 1927 in the basement of David Court below First Street, and two years later completed a center on Washington Avenue and Third Street, which soon housed a Hebrew school. The brochure goes on to note that Temple Emanu-El was organized under another name in 1940, and eight years later developed a permanent site on Washington Avenue and Seventeenth Street. Northward, on Forty-First Street, congregation Beth Sholom was organized in 1942, followed by the organization of six other congregations before 1956. That year, Miami Beach also had six synagogue schools, a Yiddish school, and an all-day Hebrew academy with an enrollment of 2,000 students.

The numbers reflect the emergence of a cohesive Jewish community within a city that became a leading vacation center in the nation. The 1956 brochure underscores an ongoing effort to develop joint curricular standards and teacher-qualification codes throughout Greater Miami. This included the sponsorship of training and seminar courses for instructors in the afternoon and weekend schools. The Greater Miami Jewish Federation made an early effort to distribute an educational subsidy among four congregations, which led to the formation in 1944 of the Bureau of Jewish Education of Greater Miami. By the early 1950s, twenty-six synagogal and full-time Orthodox schools were affiliated with the Bureau.

Serving adults, a Jewish Centers Association coordinated the activities of local Ys, leading to the formation of the Greater Miami Jewish Center in 1951. Miami Beach now also had branches of Hadassah, Mizrachi, Pioneer Women, the American Jewish Congress, Farband, and the Workmen's Circle. Yiddish stage productions were part of the Beach's cultural milieu. In 1948, Miami Beach had a Jewish mayor, Marcie Liberman, who proclaimed a Zion Day honoring the emergent state of Israel.

My study of the work of the Greater Miami Jewish Federation had particular relevance for my later appointment as research director for the New York Federation. The state of Florida had a number of Hebrew benevolent societies, going back to the 1870s, which soon were unable to cope with needs of infirm and aged visitors during colder seasons that local chambers of commerce happily referred to as "peak winter estimates" of population. The Federation in Greater Miami was launched in 1938-1939, and initially raised $80,650. By 1955, a combined appeal netted a million and a quarter dollars, which still was not enough to meet the needs of elderly and fragile Jews throughout eighteen municipalities in Dade County.

In its first pages, the 1956 brochure looked to the continuing growth, at the same pace, of the Jewish community of Miami Beach. This was overly optimistic as the city did not continue to attract the number of residents and vacationers that characterized its earlier years. Indeed, synagogue attendance, organizational memberships, and hotel registrations declined. Among visitors, the city now draws almost as many youthful tourists as elderly "snowbirds." The Jewish population continues to shift northward toward Fort Lauderdale. The brochure summarizes the character of Miami back at it high watermark in the 1950s.

> The constant influx of a great number of visitors has given special character to the local Jewish institutions. The synagogues have the highest rate of "out-of-town" attendance in the nation. Youth programs are designed to provide "a home away from home." Welfare and service organizations must take into account the needs of sojourners. There is a parallel between the mood of the hotel belt and the unprecedented emphasis placed upon educational values by the resident Jewish groups. It has been noted that in view of the fact that Miami Beach attracts Jewish communal leaders from all over the nation, local organizations have had a special relationship to national bodies.

At this point in these pages of my life, there developed in 1956–1957 a strong peripheral interest in writing creative drama for television. This interest continued actively for many years, to which I will devote a later chapter in this volume. Alongside my evolving organizational and governmental service and fundraising, I wrote a television play, titled *Ticket to Tripani,* about an Italian immigrant who won a raffle ticket for a trip to Sicily. This promptly embroiled him with members of his family who had other priorities, including planning for his daughter's wedding. He was temporarily dissuaded from the journey as other family matters took hold of him. It all became quite unbearable as dreams of the land of his origin and a desire to escape the daily humdrum of his labors pressed down upon him. At the end, he shouted, "Let me have my ticket!"

I submitted the script to the William Morris Agency in New York, which promptly had me sign a contract for representation. My agent, Bill Hart, made a determined effort to market the script, to no avail. Over the years, other screenplays evolved.

HERBERT H. LEHMAN

With ongoing studies of selected communities, my work with the American Jewish History Center continued until 1958. That year, my mentor, Professor

Allan Nevins, undertook a biography of Herbert Lehman, former governor of New York State and member of the United States Senate from 1950 to 1956. As research assistant for the biography, I became a member of Lehman's staff, which was then engaged in the movement to reform the Democratic Party in New York City.

This for me was another turning point in my life and career. It was further demonstration of how capacity as an academic researcher and writer can shape a career in organizational, governmental, and fundraising activities. These are services that a college teaching career at a far-off campus in the Midwest would not have made possible.

My research on Herbert Lehman's life and political career delved into forty-one filing cabinets holding his papers in the New York Public Library. His service as director general of UNRRA: The Organization of World Relief, from 1942 to 1946, is recorded in numerous boxes in the United Nations Library. He also dictated an oral history memoir deposited in the library of Columbia University, and his press clippings were bound in uniform volumes kept in his apartment study. From all of these sources, I wrote an 800-page typescript manuscript, which was the basis of a published volume in 1963 by Allan Nevins, titled *Herbert H. Lehman and His Era.*

I will not attempt here, in these pages of my life, to summarize all of my research on Herbert Lehman, except for the last chapter of the book, which describes the Democratic Reform movement in New York. I joined this fight against Tammany Hall, and in 1964 was hired by Mayor F. Wagner, Jr., to prepare position papers and management reports on the city's government.

Working in Herbert Lehman's office, I observed his growing involvement in the effort of young Democrats to overthrow Tammany Hall in Manhattan. The initial effort was to remove Carmine DeSapio as party leader following his rejection of the respected attorney Thomas K. Finletter as candidate for the United States Senate in 1958. Instead, DeSapio dictated the selection of Frank S. Hogan, who had been District Attorney of Manhattan. The overwhelming victory of the Republican candidate Kenneth Keating led reform-minded Democrats to form a citizens committee whose immediate goal was to attract Mayor Robert F. Wagner, Jr., to its ranks. The future of Tammany Hall hung in the balance.

As research assistant to Herbert Lehman, I was also a part of initial efforts to organize reform Democratic clubs in election districts in Manhattan. Lehman was increasingly involved in this effort. At a press conference on January 22, 1959, he, Mrs. Eleanor Roosevelt, and Finletter outlined the objectives of the New York Committee for Democratic Voters:

> To encourage the widest possible participation by all Democrats in Party affairs
> and, in furtherance of this purpose, to propose legislative and other measures

(a) to achieve democratization of the Party at all local levels, and (b) to abolish the many existing artificial barriers that now hinder participation in our Party's affairs.

The Democratic Party primary in September 1959 saw a substantial increase in both the number of voters and anti-Tammany ballots. While DeSapio won in his Greenwich Village district, and survived as chairman of the Manhattan county committee, he was pressured to announce his own plan for the rehabilitation of the party organization. In the upcoming 1960 national presidential campaign, involving the Democrat John F. Kennedy versus Vice President Richard M. Nixon, the local reform Democrats gained new strength.

The year 1961 was a turning point in the battle for control of the Democratic Party in New York City. Still employed by Herbert Lehman, I continued to be actively involved in the reform movement. A critical change in the local political scene was the alignment of Mayor Robert F. Wagner, Jr. with the reform forces, when he came out for Edward Dudley for the post of borough president of Manhattan against the Tammany regular. Wagner himself ran for reelection as mayor in the fall. I served as assistant to the deputy campaign manager, Julius C. C. Edelstein, preparing position papers on a variety of issues at campaign headquarters in the Astor Hotel and the archives at the nearby New York Times building. The campaign involved a battle for control within the Democratic Party, as well as opposition to the Republican mayoral candidate, Louis J. Lefkowitz.

I accompanied Herbert Lehman at some of his appearances in the campaign, including a trip to Coney Island and a long trek on the boardwalk. Primary Day, September 7, brought a crushing defeat of Tammany, including the ouster of DeSapio as district leader in Greenwich Village. When Robert F. Wagner, Jr. went on to gain reelection as mayor of the city, his campaign manager, Edward F. Cavanagh, replaced DeSapio as head of the Manhattan county organization. The door was now open to me to serve in the mayor's office.

Before turning to my initial service in city government, the pages in my life also include other applications of writing and marketing interests, exemplified by my 1957 contract with the William Morris Agency.

My father at this point came to me with an idea for an anti-skid, traction-increasing device for vehicles, which now had to be put in writing for presentation to a patent attorney. The device, mounted on the underside of an automobile or tractor, would contact the surface of a roadway or land surface. Upon the skidding of a vehicle, the auto-rollers would rotate in a direction opposite to that of the wheels to counteract the skidding. A United States patent is dated September 16, 1958. This is the same year that I began research for the biography of Herbert Lehman, as well as my active involvement in the Democratic reform movement.

These activities took time away from the effort to market the patent, particularly in the tractor industry, and the concept was never sold. The stretch from concept to sale was also insurmountable in regard to my father's patents for a pressurized ballpoint pen and a moveable handle for a cooking utensil.

FREEDOM IN CRISIS AMERICA

Throughout the 1950s, as covered in these pages, America was gripped by a hysterical assault upon freedom of speech and the press by the U.S. House Un-American Activities Committee and Senator Joe McCarthy of Wisconsin. The activities of intellectuals in organizations and journalism were also subject to inspection by these defenders of our nation against the Red Menace tied to the Soviet Union. I responded with an article, "Freedom in Crisis America" in *The Reconstructionist* magazine on December 18, 1953. Ironically, Professor Henry S. Commager, who read a newspaper during my oral examination to qualify for doctoral studies at Columbia, wrote to me suggesting that I continue to publish in a range of periodicals.

My article traces challenges to our nation's Bill of Rights back to the Alien and Sedition Acts of 1798, directed against Jeffersonian defenders of the original ideals of the French Revolution, which at that point had lost much of the spirit of liberté and egalité. Indeed, warships directed by the French Directory had then attacked American vessels on the high seas. Alexander Hamilton supported the Alien and Sedition Act as necessary measures to counter the "disgusting spectacle of the French Revolution."

The next major curb on constitutional liberties took place during the Civil War, when President Abraham Lincoln in 1862 denied *habeas corpus* to Northerners arrested for pro-Southern sympathies and activities. Yet, the Lincoln administration had failed to clearly define treason or its own wartime powers under the Constitution. My article notes the activities of the "Peace Democrats" who were accused of abetting the rebellious "Copperheads" in the North. In 1866, the Supreme Court expressed the view that nothing was more pernicious than the suspension of constitutional rights "during any of the great exigencies of government."

Yet, during World War I, President Woodrow Wilson stigmatized criticism of his war policy as "pro-German." When the Socialist Morris Hillquit ran for the mayoralty of New York on a peace platform in the fall of 1917, he was attacked by his opponents as a traitor. My article poses the question of where we may draw a line between criticism and sedition when America is in crisis.

This had particular relevance as Americans confronted an "age of danger," as described by President Dwight Eisenhower.

My response in my article is that ends do not justify attacks upon the Bill of Rights. I wrote: "Overt action or express proof that the stated advocacy of the forcible overthrow of the government was specifically intended to encourage overt action seems to be a clear line for the distinction between criticism and sedition." I added that "unfettered judicial authority" must be the final arbiter. Accordingly, at the time, the McCarthyite and FBI pursuit of radicals was almost totally unwarranted. I concluded the article by writing:

> A definitive criterion of sedition, upheld by all agencies for investigation and review as well as an enlightened public, shall be no bar to freedom in Crisis America.

This continues to be a major issue in the United States.

Chapter Four

City Government/Other Activities

OFFICE OF URBAN STUDIES–CITY UNIVERSITY

In my initial foray into studies of New York City government, in 1964 I served as consultant at the Office of Urban Studies, City University of New York. I drafted a series of proposals for the establishment of institutes at the City University for the study of New York City finances, the coordination of city government research, urban studies information, and state constitutional convention information.

Lacking funding for the development of a range of these institutes, the Office of Urban Studies undertook selected studies on its own initiative, which did not fully materialize. Later, the City of New York developed study programs under the aegis of the Mayor's Office. This in turn led to the formation of public commissions and citizens organizations to analyze major public issues. Now the CUNY Graduate Center has a Center for Urban Research, and Baruch College maintains a School for Public Affairs. Some of my earlier visions have come to fruition.

OFFICE OF DEPUTY MAYOR–CITY ADMINISTRATOR

In 1964, I also began working in the Office of Deputy Mayor-City Administrator as senior consultant. The office sought to develop operations research and reporting systems to strengthen the Mayor's Office in its response to a range of managerial demands. This involved the planning of actions, the monitoring of operations, and the evaluation of services performed.

34

As senior consultant, my responsibilities included administrative research and reporting, the preparation of mayoral position papers, and the development of management reports in connection with the operations of a range of City bureaus and public benefit corporations. My efforts continued through 1965 with modest results in the face of bureaucratic resistance to major changes recommended by a central agency. The legacy of the City Administrator's Office was a number of major published studies that remained relevant for many decades

TEMPORARY COMMISSION ON CITY FINANCES

As Director of Special Studies for the Commission in 1965–1966, I developed reports on City agency personnel policy, electronic data processing, the public transportation authorities, and City expenditures mandated by the state. These reports were incorporated in the Final Report of the Temporary Commission titled *Better Financing for New York City*. The directors of the Temporary Commission were Earl B. Schwulst, chairman, and Joseph D. McGoldrich, secretary.

Regarding the city's personnel system, we strongly recommended a comprehensive reorganization to facilitate municipal collective bargaining, and called for the creation of an Office of Collective Bargaining. We advised that the office ought to review fringe benefit policies and work to integrate "prevailing rate employees" into the municipal personnel structure. As the largest employer in the metropolitan area, we suggested that the city abide by certain limitations in the growing number of its employees and related personnel costs. Other cost savings could be brought about by improvements in administrative procedures and better training for personnel ranging from the executive to clerical levels.

In addition to the creation of a Collective Bargaining Office, we proposed the establishment of an Employee Relations Office to handle union negotiations, particularly in regard to wages, fringe benefits, and pensions. Our analyses dealt with such issues as prevailing rate salaries, comparing city and private sector wage levels, and recommended the abolition of prevailing rate criteria in favor of a "career and salary plan." We also made recommendations seeking to equalize fringe benefits among city departments, and called for improvements in the management of pensions-based criteria including annual rates of pay and years of service.

I proposed a report on the application of electronic data processing (EDP) for the improvement of municipal operations and controls. At the dawn of the era of the computer, I strongly advocated a large expansion in the application of EDP in relation to payroll, inventory control, appropriations account-ing, personnel records, work performance analysis, revenue collection, and information retrieval. I saw the need for interdepartmental reliance on joint computer operations with the development of centralized computer pools to bring improvements in a broad range of services.

The *Final Report* of the Temporary Commission on City Finances (1966) anticipated the role of computer in city governmental operations:

> . . . the guidance offered centrally to the City's EDP users by the Budget Bu-reau and other technical resources might well shift emphasis from equipment problems to broader policy advice on data systems. . . . Cooperation with State and Federal agencies and private organizations in EDP use, now just beginning, should be further explored and whenever possible enlarged. The possible gains from cooperation in such fields as economic research, law enforcement, and tax collection are substantial.

In another report to the Temporary Commission, I dealt with the city's relations with the semi-autonomous public transportation authorities, includ-ing the Triborough Bridge Authority and the Transit Authority. These public benefit corporations incurred annual deficits, which had to be covered by the City. My report stressed the need for a more effective city role in major decisions by these corporations in transportation development, pricing, and services. I recommended that the City's proposed transportation administra-tor should serve ex-officio as chairman of the Triborough and Transit boards, and that the Mayor should have power of review of major authority actions.

The 1966 *Final Report* of the Temporary Commission advised: "Another advantage stemming directly from greater City involvement might be more attention to increasing revenues and to holding down costs through more open competitive bidding on construction contracts, issuance of debt, and leases. Also, tolls, fares, and other charges would be set with greater concern about their effect on the whole transportation system."

STATE STUDY COMMISSION FOR NEW YORK CITY

For the State Study Commission, in 1972, I prepared a lengthy report on the reorganization of public overhead and line agencies in the allocation of ser-vices. My basic premise was that the pyramidal centralization of power in the management of these agencies should be reduced through the input of citizens in decision-making. This relates to my participation in the Democratic reform movement in the late 1950s when clubs were formed in local districts in op-position to the dictates of party bosses.

A published report issued in 1972 by the State Study Commission for New York City, titled *Restructuring the Government of New York City,* prepared by Edward N. Costikyan and Maxwell Lehman, states:

> The City Administrator Office has been weakened in recent years, and has in fact never attained the vitality originally contemplated for it. The reason is that mayors are able to use it for whatever purpose they wish. The City Administrator's Office should become what it was originally intended to be– the major managerial instrument of municipal government. It should perform continuing studies for the improvement of governmental operations.

My reports to the Commission underscored the need to develop a two-level service delivery structure in New York City government with sufficient flexibility to expand local input in agency operations. I advised that civil service personnel should cooperate with local units to build citizen participation in elected local councils. These councils would help manage such basic functions as street cleaning, street repair, housing code enforcement, local park maintenance, and personal social services. My reports stressed the need for input by the residents of established neighborhoods, and recognition of the economic condition and service requirements of different parts of the city.

A case in point is the structure of the Police Department. The report of the State Study Commission did not recommend decentralizing the department as a whole. Yet, it advised that local districts should have a significant role in the maintenance of public safety. The report recommended "that local districts be authorized, under police direction and control, to supplement police services with local residents, private guards, and other significant means." Meanwhile, established police district lines would be synchronized with changes in the delineation of neighborhood boundaries under the jurisdiction of newly established local councils.

STATE CHARTER REVISION COMMISSION

In 1972–1975, I also served as a research consultant to the State Charter Revision Commission for New York City, headed by Roy M. Goodman and Edward N. Costikyan, which substantially adopted the recommendations of the 1972 State Study Commission for New York City.

The Charter Revision Commission supported a plan for administrative decentralization designed to strengthen the managerial capacity of agencies at the borough and community levels. It called on voters to increase opportunities for citizen participation in government by strengthening community boards in the areas of planning, budgeting, and service evaluation.

On November 4, 1975, voters in New York City approved amendments to the City Charter, including the expansion of the role of community boards in establishing budget priorities, delineating service needs, and the disseminating of information regarding City services. At the same time, a major shortcoming of the charter-revision effort was the failure to deal with the semi-autonomous Public Benefit Corporations in New York City.

The Public Benefit Corporations (PBCs) are semi-private organizations set up to carry out activities where city government agencies were perceived as being inefficient. The PBCs are not subject to state and local debt limitations. Their activities range from mass transit operations; the construction of hospitals, housing, and public college facilities; and the delivery of health care services. Among these corporations are the Port Authority of New York and New Jersey, the Triborough Bridge and Tunnel Authority, and the United Nations Development Corporation. In 1975, twenty-six Public Benefit Corporations were active in New York City.

My report deals with the issue of whether the City should have greater control or influence in the activities of these corporations, including the Metropolitan Transportation Authority, which operates the City's subways and buses. A vital step would be to enact changes in the City Charter, including the creation of an Office of Intergovernmental Relations to monitor the activities of the PBCs.

In a summary of my report, I recommended that the State Charter Revision Commission should take cognizance of these corporations in regard to

- The need for greater coordination of the planning of construction activities of the city and similar activities of PBCs, including mechanisms and procedures for setting priorities as between city projects and projects of the corporations.
- The need for full disclosure of information on activities of the PBCs.
- Corporation payments to the city in lieu of real estate tax payments.
- Procedures for granting city funds and property to some PBCs and city auditing over their expenditures.
- Mayoral appointments to corporation boards.

My report addresses these issues at length. Initially, I classified the PBCs on the basis of those operating solely within New York City; others conducting regional operations; and PBCs formed for State purposes yet invited to function within New York City. In terms of their relationship to New York City, I classified the PBCs on the basis of the Mayor's power of appointment to their governing boards, the City's auditing powers, and City obligations to provide financial support (including the Transit Authority and the Health and

Hospitals Corporation). In their financial operations, my report notes that the PBCs may sell bonds in the absence of any trading powers. At the same time, the PBCs are exempt from paying real estate taxes. I indicate that the Port Authority had leased the city-owned JFK and La Guardia airports, and invested heavily in the development of these facilities. The Port Authority also proceeded–with bi-state approval and without full clearance by the City–to build the World Trade Center in lower Manhattan, which was completely destroyed on September 11, 2001, by Islamic terrorists. The City has not as yet been fully compensated for expenditures incurred in repairing damage to adjacent City property caused by the fallen buildings.

In general, the PBCs have had a massive impact on New York City finances, ranging from the construction of vital facilities independent of City funding to the City's loss of revenue from user charges and the tax exemption of these corporations. At the same time, PBC-operated hospitals and transit facilities receive partial City funding. This is partially balanced by PBC payments to the City "in lieu of taxes." Accordingly, my report underscores the need for expanded coordination and joint planning.

I recommended the creation of a mechanism to promote City coordination with the PBCs. I advised that the City's Charter Revision Commission should call on the state legislature to authorize such a coordinating body to be known as the Office of Intergovernmental Relations, to be administered at the Deputy Mayor level. I wrote:

> Office functions might include ongoing review, in behalf of the city, of the activities of PBCs for the purpose of promoting joint city and PBC planning objectives. The Office, as projected, could play an integral role in institutionalizing joint city-PBC practices, in evaluating local PBC operations, and in providing liaison for the development of unified services. The proposed office would be responsible for developing "memorandums of understanding" with PBCs operating in the city, which would deal with funding, the ongoing joint review of the status of projects, and the coordination of a broad range of operational functions.

My report goes on to deal with mayoral appointments to the boards of PBCs operating exclusively in the city. I suggested that the Mayor's annual message to the City Council should have a specific section dealing with the PBCs to increase public awareness of their activities in the city. In accordance with the public's right to know, I recommended that all relevant reports and documents be distributed to local city officials whose agencies are impacted by PBC projects. I suggested that all formal decisions of PBC boards should be publicized: "PBCs should be required to notify community boards or successor bodies, in advance, of programs, projects, or facilities planned for local areas."

On the transfer of City property to PBCs, such as the lease of the local major airports to the Port Authority, I advised that the public should be informed at an early stage regarding such proposed transfers. This would be well in advance of final consideration by the city's Board of Estimate.

My report deals with City appropriations to Public Benefit Corporations, such as advances to cover the costs of the Transit Police Force. I recommended that such allocations be fully reviewed by the City Comptroller. I also suggested that PBC tolls and fares be subject to full public scrutiny. "As a condition of the city's appropriation of funds and the transfer of city property to PBCs, the city charter might require the Board of Estimate to obtain the agreement of affected corporations to report annually all information on specific sources of revenue."

I also called for a comprehensive review of PBC payments to the City in lieu of taxes, particularly in regard to property leased to private tenants conducting businesses for profit. I suggested that formulas be developed on the amortization of individual PBC facilities as a basis for the renegotiation of voluntary agreements for payments in lieu of taxes.

In general, my report recommends that the expansion of the PBCs be limited through the establishment by New York City of local development corporations, which would combine features of the PBCs, and the capital programs of public agencies. I noted that the State Constitution authorizes municipalities to expand debts outside their debt limits to the extent that capital projects are self-sustaining. At the time, I pointed to the New York City Public Development Corporation–a nonprofit agency designed to make more of the city's land available for industrial development–as a certain model for the proposed local development corporations.

These proposed local corporations would have the right to acquire, lease, or sell property; to fix and collect uniform rates and other charges to maintain operations on a self-sustaining basis; and to borrow money, issue negotiable loans, and execute contracts. The corporations could become eligible to receive City appropriations and lease property from the City. They would be subject to City audit, and would be required to make full disclosure of information on their operations.

As this review of my report on the PBCs was being written, there appeared an article in *The New York Times* on July 22, 2009, with the headline, "Lawmakers Move to Reform State's Public Authorities." The State Senate passed an act to make the PBCs more accountable to oversight by a state budget office. Contracts awarded by the PBCs over $1 million would have to be reviewed by the state comptroller, and new limits would be placed on them in their issuance of debt.

Assemblyman Richard L. Brodsky of Westchester County sponsored the bill, declaring the PBCs are "secretive; they're run by commissions. Sometimes they do the right thing and sometimes they don't, but no one knows." He noted that the Metropolitan Transportation Authority ran $300 million over budget in building its headquarters with no-bid contracts, leading to criminal investigations. On November 18, 2009, the New York State Assembly approved a further measure for stricter oversight of the approximately 700 state authorities.

Before returning to my variegated career—which for many years saw me as a development officer for voluntary, nonprofit organizations—I turn once again to my wife's service in relation to new immigrants and early childhood education.

In 1962, we moved to the Riverdale section of The Bronx. Naomi promptly conducted Yiddish press analyses for the Nationalities Division of Citizens for Kennedy in the presidential race. This followed her work, ten years earlier, as interviewer of Jewish immigrants for the volume, *Life Is with People,* and service as case worker with the New York Association for New Americans. Certified in Early Childhood Education, my wife moved on to be a kindergarten teacher in a Yonkers public school and the Inwood Nursery School.

Later, in 1969, she was appointed director of the B'nai Jeshurun Nursery School in Manhattan, and in 1972 began as head of the Nursery School of the Riverdale YM-YWHA. Naomi was a member of the Executive Committee of the Early Childhood Teachers Association of the Board of Jewish Educators. In 1976–1977, she was creator, writer, and narrator for "Shalom Corner," a 13-part television series on Jewish early education for pre-school children. In 1982, she was nursery school director for the Jewish Community Center on the Palisades, in Tenafly, New Jersey.

I remained as senior consultant, Office of Deputy Mayor—City Administrator through 1965, but was not retained by John V. Lindsay, who was elected that year as Republican mayor of the City. I was promptly hired in December by the United Parents Associations, then in the throes of a sharply declining membership of middle-class parents of pupils in the public schools. The central office could not raise its operational costs, and in 1967 I was again looking for a position.

FEDERATION OF JEWISH PHILANTHROPIES OF NEW YORK

At this point, my career took a turn, as a source of livelihood, from research on governmental issues to fundraising in support of nonprofit organizations and universities. I continued my involvement as consultant on issues confronting the City of New York, while my focus was increasingly directed to obtaining foundation and government grants to support institutional budgets for general operations and special projects. In 1967, I was employed as Director, Research Department, Federation of Jewish Philanthropies of New York. The executive vice president of Federation was David G. Salten, and Peter L. Malkin was chairman of the committee on research.

In addition to reporting on a range of research projects conducted by agencies in the field, I analyzed fundraising activities at Federation's headquarters. This was central to providing financial support for all agency programs. From 1967 to 1969, I issued an annual *Research Reporter* summarizing my studies of headquarters operations and reports prepared by affiliate agencies.

I initially found that the Federation headquarters' fundraising record-keeping system was severely limited, which made the analysis of data extremely difficult. Another study discerned that among a select number of top Jewish business executives in New York, more than half the individuals or firms did not contribute to Federation. I provided the names of 2,000 Jewish non-donors/small donors for a proposed special solicitation effort. A similar study of 765 Jewish-sponsored foundations identified a substantial number to be approached for first-time or increased grants. Another study, based on my interview of 40 large donors, suggested criteria for maintaining or increasing gifts to Federation. Other studies in my first year as research director dealt with the employment of auxiliary workers, the work of the New Leadership Division, and campaign dinner costs.

In 1968, I contacted ninety-two Federation agencies and affiliates on their Jewish/non-Jewish intake and services, and found that a quarter of their patients and clients were not Jewish. Since most of the agencies were also receiving public funds, their admissions had to be nonsectarian. Accordingly, I showed that Federation's service agencies were making a vital contribution to New York's general population. My other reports in 1968 dealt with the aged Jewish population and the availability of long-term care facilities, and the costs of fundraising events.

In 1968–1970, a report dealt with the estimated Jewish population of city community mental health catchment areas, which noted an increasing number of elderly Jews. Two studies analyzed the growing utilization of paraprofessionals in social services, and reviewed training programs for these personnel. Another report described the growing number of programs for Jewish senior citizens in a range of local synagogues and community centers. Other studies compared Federation and local university endowment fund programs, and contributions to Federation by medical staffs.

In a letter to Peter Malkin on January 24, 1969, the executive vice president, David G. Salten, wrote:

In my first annual report as executive vice president, I underscored the importance of the research effort for Federation, and my satisfaction with the quality and scope of the Committee's work, which I have been following closely. Federation's top volunteer and professional leadership have also reviewed the reports, and have taken important steps to implement the findings and recommendations . . .

Chapter Five

Fundraising

In 1968, a deep split developed within the New York Federation between the fundraising departments and the social work sections. The vituperative, antagonistic Director of Community Services, Martha K. Selig, led an assault against the executive vice president demanding that headquarters should now direct more attention to the delivery of community and mental health services. After accomplishing many changes in the organization's fundraising, David F. Salten was forced out of his post in 1969. My own days at Federation, with emphasis on the raising of funds, were now numbered.

The new vice president of Federation, Sanford Solender, hired through Martha Selig, paid more attention to the delivery of social services now that sufficient funding was forthcoming. My days at headquarters were running out because I did not have a degree in social work. I began looking at local universities for a development position, with my solid qualifications. On the basis of a doctorate in history, I could write strong fundraising proposals, and I had extensive experience in government to be able to relate to federal and foundation personnel.

FORDHAM UNIVERSITY

In 1971, I started with Fordham University as Associate Director of Development, at its campus next to Lincoln Center. I promptly obtained a $500,000 grant from the Andrew W. Mellon Foundation for support of liberal arts studies at the mid-Manhattan campus. The president of the Jesuit-sponsored university, Father James C. Finlay, remarked publicly how gratifying it was to receive such a gift to ease the financial burdens of the school. My secret thought was that it was also felicitous that a Jewish fundraiser had a key role in a Catholic institution.

In the next two years, I also obtained grants of $100,000 from the Charles Hayden Foundation for Fordham's athletic center and $88,000 from the Rockefeller Foundation for support of graduate training in public social services for minority-group social workers.

I organized a foundation committee and contacted over 250 Fordham Law School alumni whose associates served as officers of leading foundations for the submission of proposals for major grants. Smaller gifts were also received for general operating support from a range of foundations throughout the United States. I drafted a University case statement and collaborated in the preparation of a booklet on deferred giving.

To obtain support for the construction of a gymnasium at Fordham's Rose Hill campus in the Bronx, I visited Green Bay, Wisconsin, to solicit funds from the Green Bay Packers football team. This professional team had been coached by Vincent T. Lombardi, a Fordham graduate and football linesman who had been one of the team's "seven blocks of granite" in the 1930s. The new athletic center was to be named for him.

With his widow, I also visited President Richard Nixon in the White House, where we were ushered into the Chief Executive's private office. On my apartment wall today, I have a photograph that shows me shaking hands with Nixon. I have always been amused by the thought that physically and emotionally this was as high that a "kid from the Bronx" could go.

But I did not obtain the post of Director of Development at Fordham, which went to a Catholic fundraiser without proposal writing skills, who was retained for two years. In the interim, I left for another development position. At the same time, a pattern was emerging in my career, marked by success in non-tenured employment and a personal commitment to principles which at times conflicted with the pragmatic actions of organizational executives. I increasingly took on consultantships, with various titles, in government and fundraising, and offered my services under the name J R Productions. I stressed my research and writing skills and record of obtaining large grants for a range of non-profit organizations.

PHOENIX HOUSE

In 1974–1975, I was employed by Dr. Mitchell Rosenthal at Phoenix House in New York City to obtain funding for its anti-narcotics activities. I prepared and successfully marketed a proposal for support of the treatment of problem adolescents in an open-intake therapeutic center. Located on the West Side of

Manhattan near a public square referred to as "Needle Park," Phoenix House expanded its group therapeutic meetings for a growing number of afflicted young people. I also obtained funding for Phoenix House's care of prisoners and parolees in a joint prison-halfway house therapeutic community.

The grants I obtained contributed significantly to the expansion of Phoenix House services throughout the City. Over time, the organization launched therapeutic centers in new quarters in Brooklyn, Queens, the Bronx, and other parts of Manhattan. An Ambulatory School Program and Cocaine Hotline further extended the organization's services.

ALLERGY FOUNDATION OF AMERICA

In 1975, I also worked for the Allergy Foundation in the expansion of its fundraising and public relations programs. I initiated corporate and foundation solicitations with a funding proposal backed by letter and telephone appeals. Board members appeared on radio and television programs, and I started the computerization of the organization's mailing list. To broaden the group's appeal, I advised that its name be changed to Asthma and Allergy Foundation as it is now known, based in Washington, D.C.

CITIZENS BUDGET COMMISSION

In 1975, I prepared and presented three foundation proposals on behalf of the Citizens Budget Commission (New York City). These appeals dealt with the financing of local courts, a review of the costs of daycare programs, and a study of the City's sources of revenue for support of these services.

My review of the City's budget in relation to the courts and daycare found there was ongoing resort to massive borrowing to meet ongoing expenses, as well as the use of capital funds to help pay for operating costs. I advocated that there be greater input by citizen groups and City Council members in the review of mayoral projections of the cost of programs and the personnel required to run them. I suggested the creation of an independent City board for budgeting and the development of spending alternatives.

In connection with the budget process, I called for greater input by the City Council in the formulation of the City's budget, including expanded public hearings and restrictions on the Mayor's veto powers. I suggested that the City Comptroller work more closely with the City Council. I also recommended that the Council be given post-audit powers, including the determination of changes in specific program appropriations following approval of the budget. My proposals also suggested that large sections of the expense and capital budgets be combined since capital borrowing was being used to help finance operating costs.

My proposals also supported the creation of a State Financing Bank to help localities in the marketing of bonds to meet the operating costs of courts, daycare centers, and other services. The proposed State Bank would emulate the Federal Financing Bank to reduce the number of agency financing personnel dealing with the securities markets and to build expertise in connection with complex debt-management operations. A central financing facility, I stressed, would lower interest and underwriting costs, and assure an adequate flow of credit. The facility would work closely with the State Comptroller in dealing with obligations issued and guaranteed by a locality. I advised that the Citizens Budget Commission should analyze the impact of the proposed State Financing Bank on New York City's debt service costs and cash flow problems. I suggested that analyses of the cost of operating the courts and daycare centers would serve as examples for the overhaul of a broad range of City fiscal operations.

My three proposals for the Citizens Budget Commission recommended discreet cuts in the city's appropriations for public services to reduce reliance on the capital budget to help pay for operating costs. I suggested increased user charges for daycare services and reliance on Public Benefit Corporations to take over selected City agency operations. The latter, I suggested, could issue bonds for capital construction over and above the City's debt limit and provide for the expansion of services with equitable charges.

OTHER ASSIGNMENTS: 1975

I served as advisor to Arthur Andersen & Co. (Chicago), at the time one of the largest accounting firms in the nation. I collaborated in the preparation of the firm's report to the U.S. Secretary of the Treasury on New York City finances with respect to the repayment of federal seasonal loans. This entailed a review of the City's income and expenditures, its departmental budgets, and fiscal procedures and controls. I also prepared proposals for dealing with New York City's financial planning and ongoing fiscal analyses of functional activities.

The same year, I worked at the Economic Development Council of New York City where I prepared a report on the finances of the City University of New York (CUNY). As a tuition-free complex at the time, CUNY was largely dependent on the City for its operating costs, along with extensive funding from the state for community colleges, doctoral programs, and teacher education courses. I strongly supported the continuation of CUNY as a separate entity from the State University and favored the continuation of its free-tuition policy in a city with many immigrants and low-income families. But tuition was imposed in 1975.

I supported increased State funding for CUNY's operating and capital expenditures, since the City University relieved the State University (SUNY) of a major financial outlay. Indeed, the State University has very few facilities in New York City. At the same time, my report raised questions about the cost effectiveness of CUNY's Open Admissions program. By 1999, CUNY's four-year college ended Open Admissions, which had been lowering academic levels. At the same time, graduates of the two-year community colleges have unrestricted admissions into CUNY's senior colleges.

For the Citizens Union Foundation in 1975, I analyzed City and State expenditures for employees in New York City courts, compiled data on the number of positions and salary levels in the courts, and provided information on the assignment of estates and fees to attorneys by the Surrogate Courts. Most of this was statistical and without extensive narration.

UTICA COLLEGE

After a range of advisory positions, I was ready to seek an appointment as a top administrator at a university. Earlier in this memoir, I commented on my failing efforts to obtain a teaching position in many of these institutions. In response to an advertisement, in 1976, I became Director of Development and College Relations at Utica College of Syracuse University, New York. My wife and I decided that she would remain in our New York City apartment and that we would be seeing each other on weekends.

My responsibilities in this post were based on my academic background, research directorships, analytic reports, and fundraising experience. I promptly organized eleven occupational and special support committees made up of 115 businessmen in the Utica area. These groups sought to cultivate higher-level annual support of the college along with special-purpose donations. Within months, the community's recognition of the wide-ranging needs of this college led to a substantial increase in gifts. A growing awareness of the vital role of the college in the city and its economy brought members of the fundraising committees together at joint meetings addressed by Utica mayor Edward A. Hanna and Dr. Harold J. Rankin, president of the college.

Drawing on my foundation, corporate, and government funding background, I drafted proposals for support of a range of research and demonstration projects at the college. A grant of $40,000 came from the U.S. Office of

Education, and the Louis Calder Foundation donated $20,000. I also initiated an effort to identify and cultivate of local area foundations, which yielded several smaller grants from these sources in Oneida County.

I developed endowment and deferred-giving programs, which established long-range commitments for support of the institution. Within months of my arrival, I expanded the alumni office and issued a quarterly alumni bulletin. The publications office developed brochures on college programs, and to attract a wider range of students initiated special admissions newsletters. A major objective was to draw more students from New York City.

To publicize the college, I helped bring the Duane Bobick-Chuck Wepner heavyweight championship bout to the Utica College Sports Center in 1976, televised live and nationally by ABC's network program, Wide World of Sports.

At the end of 1977, I unexpectedly received a call from a close associate of Edward I. Koch, newly elected Mayor of the City of New York, asking me to join his administration as Senior Assistant to Herman Badillo, who was to serve as Deputy Mayor for Policy. After due consideration and discussion with my wife, I decided to return to New York City.

DEPUTY MAYOR FOR POLICY

In this point in my narrative, I will briefly review my venture back into City government. As Senior Assistant to the Deputy Mayor for Policy, I drafted major reports, proposals, and analyses of City programs, including studies of City University construction and the Model Cities Program, which was an effort to assist private developers for middle-income housing. For the Deputy Mayor, I served as liaison with all City agencies, wrote speeches and press releases.

At the same time, a deep split developed between the Mayor and Badillo over the revitalization of the South Bronx, leading to the latter's departure from City government. It was soon time for me to leave the Mayor's office and I was appointed in 1979 as President of Dropsie University in Philadelphia. My job entailed a financial rescue effort, which I accomplished through 1981.

Dropsie University

The institution was established and endowed through the will of Moses Aaron Dropsie, drawn in 1895, in which he directed "that there be established in the City of Philadelphia a college for the promotion of and instruction in the

Hebrew and cognate languages and their respective literatures." After his death in 1905, a charter was granted to the facility as a postgraduate institution offering a Ph.D. degree in its disciplines, initially without tuition. The campus was then in the heart of the Jewish community on Broad Street in North Philadelphia. Over time, its library holdings and manuscript division attracted leading scholars in ancient Hebrew and biblical studies. Dropsie's first doctorate was bestowed on Bernard Revel in 1909, who became first president of Yeshiva College in New York.

By the 1970s, with the movement of the Jewish community away from the area, Dropsie University faced a sharp drop in its financial support and student attendance. In 1979, I was asked to rescue the University from bankruptcy and imminent closure as an independent institution. With an advanced degree in American History, I had little background in Dropsie's disciplines, and instead brought my experience to my mission as a fundraiser.

Surrounded by a black community, with ties to former synagogue structures now turned churches and storefront houses of worship, I sensed that Dropsie with its biblical studies could reach out to lay ministers with little formal theological training. I initially obtained grants totaling $71,000 from the William Penn Foundation and $40,000 from the Pew Memorial Trust for a Community Outreach Program. This involved employing Dropsie's faculty as instructors at classes of black ministers in biblical studies.

These sessions ranged from the Pentateuch, the history of the Bible, the Book of Genesis, Biblical Law, and Aramaic Bible Versions. At the same time, the foundation grants helped cover Dropsie's overhead expenses and faculty salaries. Then came a grant of $150,000 from The Glenmede Trust for the community outreach effort, as well as the renovation of the former Mikveh Israel synagogue building on Dropsie's campus. The foundation grants brought general attention to Dropsie's activities, as evidenced further by a $10,000 gift from the Samuel S. Fels Fund for a planned Institute for Advanced Jewish and Middle Eastern Studies.

I promptly launched a Master's degree program, and began to cultivate Walter H. Annenberg for the purchase of a building at Independence Square in Philadelphia as a new campus for Dropsie. Annenberg was publisher of the *Philadelphia Inquirer* and *Seventeen Magazine*, and had served as ambassador to Great Britain from 1969 to 1974. His gift of $5 million later financed the acquisition of a new building in the center of Philadelphia.

Prior to my departure from Dropsie in 1981, I recruited seventeen new members of the board, continued to increase the holdings of the library, and added to the number of scholarships and fellowships. Dropsie's periodical *The Jewish Quarterly Review* continues to be published as an important journal with articles and reviews on Jewish literature, history, religion, and Hebrew philology. New funding also became available for the publication of additional volumes in Dropsie's series entitled *Jewish Apocryphal Literature for the Interpretation of Judaism and Christianity.*

With seeming assurance of financial security and a continuing effort to obtain a grant from the Annenberg Foundation for a new campus building, some members of the board began to push for a new university president with a doctorate in biblical and rabbinic studies. In this, they were abetted by David M. Goldenberg, a member of the faculty, who gained the presidency, though lacking fundraising and administrative experience. It was a fateful step, which led finally to Dropsie's collapse as an independent institution.

Following my departure and Goldenberg's removal from the presidency, there was a succession of replacements, all undermined by Goldenberg. Dropsie could not continue, and the University of Pennsylvania stepped in to turn the institution into the Center for Advanced Judaic Studies.

This chain of events is a further commentary on the vital role of administrative leadership for the support of scholarly pursuits. Also, academia cannot continue without a fundraising base. My experience further demonstrates that personal self-interest must give way to concern for the well-being of an organization as a test of effective leadership.

One member of the Dropsie board expected that I continue to hire his girlfriend for six-month periods as my secretary, and made a grant to the institution exclusively to pay for her half-year employment. I encountered another leading member of the board entering the elevator in a New York hotel with a prostitute. These dominating board members would no longer tolerate my presence. I left Dropsie to join the staff of the March of Dimes Birth Defects Foundation. This appointment came about through the initiative of Dr. Samuel J. Ajl, Vice President for Research at the March of Dimes and a former member of the board of Dropsie University.

MARCH OF DIMES

The organization was established in 1938 to combat infantile paralysis through the initiative of President Franklin Roosevelt and his former law partner, Basil O'Connor. The March of Dimes financed Jonas Salk and Albert Sabin in their production of vaccines to halt this dreaded illness. In 1958, the organization transformed itself into the March of Dimes Birth Defects Foundation for the prevention of premature births and support of research into the causes of birth defects. The Catholic-oriented organization openly opposed abortion as a means of halting the birth of severely disabled babies.

I joined the organization in 1981 as assistant to President C. L. Massey. This involved a 1½ hour trip from my co-op apartment in Manhattan to White Plains by subway, railroad, and bus. In one capacity, I coordinated eight annual meetings of scientific advisory committees throughout the country for the review of applications for research support. This involved coordinating hotel reservations, sending out meeting invitations, and overseeing all arrangements at these gatherings.

PRETERM BIRTHS

By 1983, I was also able to take on a second vital role at the March of Dimes involving the preparation of applications for major foundation and government funding of a range of special research and infant-care programs. One jointly prepared proposal helped the Colonel Harland Sanders Memorial Endowment Fund at the March of Dimes reach its $1 million goal in conjunction with the Kentucky Fried Chicken food chain. The Endowment was able to expand a study of the prevention of premature births, to be conducted at six medical centers.

BASIC PREMISES

The proposal sought matching grants for clinical trials to determine whether a successful program for the prevention of premature births at the University of California-San Francisco Medical Center (UCSF) could be replicated throughout the United States. The proposed study would be based on the following premises:

- Preterm birth is the major cause of infant illness and mortality, and is the greatest challenge today in obstetric health care.
- The rate of preterm births in the United States is approximately double the rate in countries with the lowest levels of infant mortality.
- The March of Dimes-sponsored project at UCSF achieved a 73 percent reduction in the prior preterm rate at this medical center.
- A broad-based field test involving patients from widely different backgrounds is needed to apply and confirm the UCSF methods and results.
- If the preterm birth rate can be reduced by 50 percent in the United States, the saving in neonatal intensive care costs would be over a half billion dollars annually.

IMPLEMENTATION

The staff proposal noted that at the San Francisco Medical Center, new tocolytic drugs appeared to limit preterm labor, while taking into account factors of previous obstetrical history, complications of present pregnancy, age, and socioeconomic condition. UCSF found a marked reduction in admissions to the neonatal intensive care unit among infants born to high-risk mothers who received special care. In a two-year period at UCSF, there was a 73 percent reduction in the prior preterm rate. Accordingly, the March of Dimes proposed a three-year study at additional medical centers to test the general applicability of the UCSF methodology.

After three years, the evaluation of the study would include a statistical comparison of the rates of preterm birth in the experimental and control groups, and both would be compared with the rates for nonparticipants and low-risk groups. The evaluation would be objective, numerical, free of bias, and subject to statistical analysis.

RESULTS

The 1986 results of the three-year study were quite definitive and encouraging. The participating medical centers found that the prevention of preterm births clearly involved the identification of women at risk of delivering prematurely, and training them to detect the subtle early signs of labor. Also, treatment with new drugs could delay labor, if detected early enough, obtaining crucial extra time for the unborn baby. At the same time, the March of Dimes did not support abortions of severely defective fetuses.

PRENATAL NURSING CARE

While continuing to serve the March of Dimes as coordinator of meetings of the national scientific advisory committees, I personally drafted a proposal to the U.S. Department of Health and Human Services to develop core competencies in maternal/child health care in undergraduate nursing schools. A grant in 1985 of $353,000 enabled the March of Dimes to recruit participants in the project, including the American Nurses Association, the American Association of Colleges of Nursing, and the Nurses Association of the American College of Obstetricians and Gynecologists. The project aimed to develop a curriculum to prepare students to provide more effective early and continuous prenatal care to pregnant women, including those from special cultural and socioeconomic backgrounds.

RATIONALE

A basic premise of the project was that maternal/ infant morbidity and mortality needed to be addressed by the increased use of technology, the further regionalization of levels of perinatal service, and an aggressive approach to risk assessment and preventive care particularly during the first trimester. At the time, however, the severe shortage of skilled perinatal nurses limited the potential of these measures to improve pregnancy outcomes and the health of newborns. The perinatal content in schools of nursing appeared to be a root cause of the inability of the states to provide sufficient professional personnel for the technological and organizational resources that were at hand. Undergraduate instruction had to address this dichotomy by examining curriculums and teaching methodologies in maternal/child health. This effort had the potential of increasing the number of entry-level practitioners in maternal/infant nursing, as well as the number of students in perinatal graduate programs.

PROJECT GOALS

The goals of the project were the preparation and demonstration of core competencies that would: (1) Develop an understanding of the needs of special population groups that posed high-risk problems in the public health field, to increase the skill of the beginning-level practitioner in relation to diverse individual, adolescent, working women and lifestyle situations; (2) provide a theoretical and clinical basis for effective beginning-level perinatal practice to help the states meet the service and technological demands particularly of high-risk maternal/ fetal, maternal/newborn, and neonatal situations; (3) develop a sound comprehension among student nurses of the elements of assessment, planning, implementation, and evaluation in primary perinatal care programs extended through public health facilities. Another vital benefit would be the development of new curricular materials, guidebooks, and manuals as teaching aids in the education of nurses.

THREE-YEAR STUDY

In the first year, the project would survey and analyze current curriculums and teaching methodologies used in 300 baccalaureate schools of nursing to prepare students for maternal/infant nursing; develop a definition of competencies necessary for effective clinical and community-based practice; and identify those schools which had implemented a range of competencies. A panel of specialists was to be convened to define the full range of competencies, and make recommendations on the development of a survey tool that would determine what was being taught and how. The next twelve months would refine the competencies and develop a self-assessment tool for schools. These would proceed from requests for further information from schools that had incorporated a range of competencies, site visits to these schools, and another meeting of the panel. The last phase (twelve months) would include the preparation of guidelines for the implementation of the model; the convening of four regional meetings for dissemination of information; and the identification of sites for implementation of a pilot program.

DEMONSTRATION MODEL

The implementation guidelines would describe how the teaching of perinatal nursing can be incorporated in the full length of a general course of instruction, and how didactic and clinical elements should be integrated to best prepare students for early and ongoing prenatal care including services for women who customarily would have delayed or avoided such care. The core competencies framework, implementation plan, and demonstration model would be evaluated by independent specialists who would be asked to review the end products from the standpoint of content, design, applicability, and learning outcome. The project would provide to schools of nursing data and analysis on what was being taught on maternal/infant care, core competencies, a tool for self-assessment, teaching plan, and (following the three-year grant period) the results and evaluation of pilot demonstrations.

ADAPTATION OF RESULTS

My proposal concluded with a statement on the significance of the project.
  The project would provide to baccalaureate schools of nursing

- data and analysis on what is presently being taught in maternal/infant health care;
- core competencies for early and continuous prenatal care, including the care of the subgroup of women who have customarily delayed or avoided prenatal service;

- a tool for self-assessment;
- an implementation guide for schools of nursing for the development and testing of student competencies in maternal/infant health care.

On the basis of the in-kind input of the three sponsoring organizations, their various professional affiliations and periodic panel and regional meetings, sites for a pilot program would be recommended.

The core competencies structure would meet substantially unmet needs in nursing education, and might subsequently influence standards for baccalaureate schools of nursing. It would have an impact on the quality of preventive and health promotion practices, and improve pregnancy outcome in general and special population groups. The latter -- including various cultural minorities, the poor, adolescents, and working women at risk -- represented a special challenge in the public health field.

Dr. Beverly Raff, March of Dimes Vice President for Professional Education, wrote to me on December 3, 1984:

"I believe your thorough research about the need to study Maternal/Infant Nursing Curriculum and your careful preparation of the grant application were decisive factors in the positive outcome of this effort."

See Appendix for the text of the proposal.

STARTER RESEARCH GRANTS

Earlier, in April 1982, I had obtained a grant of $8,200 for the March of Dimes from the RGK Foundation for the Starter Research Grants Program. The grant was to be used for a study of gene duplication before cell division, a process where there is a potential cause of birth defects. The March of Dimes was committed to match this grant to be applied for a two-year study at a university.

Prior research about the structure and behavior of genes suggested possibilities for correcting certain major genetic diseases. Ongoing studies of human cells in laboratory culture gave promise of the saving of lives. Brain research was being revolutionized by a growing understanding of neurohormonal circuits. Scientists were also probing the network theory of immunity involving complex interactions among white blood cell subtypes and the generation of antibodies.

The RGK Foundation grant was applied to the work of Dr. Joyce L. Hamlin on gene duplication at the University of Virginia School of Medicine.

JEWISH GENETIC DISEASES

With the special interest of Dr. Samuel J. Ajl, vice president for research at the March of Dimes, I also prepared a brochure on the treatment of the Tay-Sachs, Gaucher, and Niemann-Pick diseases. The publication asked for funds to support the allocation of almost one million dollars a year by the March of Dimes for research and medical services dealing with inherited disorders prevalent among Jewish people.

In the 1980s, one in about 900 Jewish marriages was between carriers of Tay-Sachs genes. This resulted in the death of one in every 3,600 Jewish babies due to this fatal disease. These Tay-Sachs babies were born without an enzyme necessary for breaking down certain fatty deposits in brain and nerve cells. A blood test along with a study of cells in the fluid surrounding the fetus could detect the disease, but this would be too late to save affected babies after birth. The March of Dimes was searching for methods to supply the nervous system with the missing enzyme related to Tay-Sachs.

Accordingly, the brochure that I prepared sought donations for a range of research projects on Jewish genetic diseases; the delivery of related genetic and educational services; and the publication of study modules and promotional materials in the field.

At a meeting with President C. L. Massey in 1985, I was offered long-term tenure at the March of Dimes to continue my proposal writing and arrangements for national professional meetings. However, I did not wish to continue my lengthy daily commute and ongoing out-of-town trips. Nor did I wish to adapt my written materials to the organization's anti-abortion stand.

Instead, I chose to become an independent businessman, from 1986 to 1990, for fundraising and the placement of administrative, fundraisers, and public relations personnel in nonprofit organizations. I volunteered extensively in the political activities of Herman Badillo, in support of Democratic candidates for presidential nominations, including his own defeated race in 1986 for New York State Comptroller.

At this point in my memoir, I am returning to family matters, with emphasis on the marital lives of my two daughters.

My daughter Joyce's first marriage in the 1970s lasted briefly. In December 1981, Joyce married Rabbi Lionel Moses from Toronto, Canada.

Rabbi Moses had majored in chemistry and then earned a Master's degree in Ancient Near Eastern Studies from the University of Toronto. In 1977, he was ordained a Rabbi at the Jewish Theological Seminary in New York, and served a congregation in Mamaroneck, New York. After his marriage, he was rabbi at Conservative synagogues in Jackson Heights (Queens) and Sacramento, California, where my daughter was an English professor at Chapman University. They have three boys. Zev and Jeremy were born in New York in 1983 and 1986. Ezra was born in Sacramento in 1990.

My son-in-law served many years on the Seminary's Committee on Jewish Law and Standards, also as Secretary of the Joint Beth Din of the Conservative Movement, and sits on the Joint Placement Commission of the Rabbinical Assembly and the United Synagogue of Conservative Judaism. Rabbi Moses was president of the Montreal Board of Rabbis, and corresponding secretary of the North American Board of Rabbis.

My younger daughter Ruth has continued her long-term position as conference manager for the Education Development Center in Newton, Massachusetts. In August 1992, she married Peter Wetherbee who had come to the Boston area from Ohio. Peter was in music sales, and remains an accomplished folksinger with weekly engagements. After extensive preparation, he became a graphic designer, and is now employed by Cambridge College with responsibility for all its student recruitment publications. They have one son, Benjamin, who was born in 1994.

Random memories of the 1980s include my effort in 1983 to visit Dr. Jonas Salk of polio vaccine fame at his San Diego Salk Institute office, without appointment. This was after the March of Dimes turned its efforts from fighting polio to overcoming birth defects, and I was with the organization at the time. His secretary spoke to him directly, and he declined to see me. Probably he still had questions about the organization's support of Dr. Albert B. Sabin's subsequent development of a live oral vaccine against polio.

Glimpses from my memories of 1985 recall a visit to Jack Leopold in Mountain View, California. He was my mother's relative in Poland, who fought the German occupiers and their Polish cohorts during World War II. As a partisan, Jack survived in the woods outside his hometown. At one point, he entered the town alone to seek his family, who were gone. Hungry and bedraggled, he turned to a priest on the street, who invited him into the church for sustenance until his return to the forests.

As a volunteer in Herman Badillo's 1986 campaign for the State Comptroller's office, I recall the expressions of gratitude by one of the Hispanic secretaries for my patient handling of her repeated mistakes in the typing of a document.

In May 1987, at the large reunion of young people who grew up in the Sholem Aleichem Houses, which Ruth Singer and I had helped organize, I encountered Violet Newman, my childhood heartthrob. She said she married "a boy from the neighborhood." I then asked her if I might kiss her goodnight, and she said I could as my wife stood nearby.

CONGREGATION ADATH JESHURUN

In 1986, I was employed as campaign director at Congregation Adath Jeshurun in Elkins Park, Pennsylvania. This was an endowment fund drive organized by the Milton Ward Company, with offices in Baldwin, New York. The campaign involved the solicitation of some twenty-five Challenge Gift prospects for grants of $100,000 and over, as well as a range of gifts at lower levels. This was my first experience with non-foundation funding, and reliance on membership donations obtained by pledges. Categories of donations, with percentages of expected grants toward a $4 million campaign goal, were divided as follows:

Challenge Gifts	12–14	40%
Leadership Gifts	120	30%
Advance Gifts	300	20%
General Gifts	500	10%

The campaign involved informational meetings for volunteers on reaching out to over 1,200 family congregants in connection with the four gift levels. Emphasis was placed on inaugurating a tuition-free religious school, to be supported by the endowment fund, as a means of halting the erosion of congregational membership and attracting new families. Pledged gifts were to be payable over five years, and donor names were to be entered on an endowment wall in the main lobby of the synagogue.

On my part, the intensive two-month start-up effort meant the drafting of the campaign brochure in cooperation with synagogal leadership and the Milton Ward organization. Volunteers required instruction on solicitation procedures based on learning about prospects' interests and capacity for giving. Solicitors needed to be thoroughly grounded in all aspects of goals of the campaign. Underscoring this effort was the need to obtain firm pledges of gift amounts based on a mutual understanding of a "fair share" donation.

For me, this fundraising experience directed to individual giving was an extension of my proposal-writing background based on specific foundation interests. I learned about the importance of preserving an institution in lieu of obtaining funding for a specific project.

This commitment to the advancement of an institution was expressed in the campaign brochure, which I helped write:

> Although it has already achieved excellence, today's Adath Jeshurun still seeks
> it. It is engaged in a process that is as much distinguished by effort as it is by

success. There is everywhere and every day a perpetual striving to provide the most meaningful services, the most effective education, the warmest possible communal home. There is an uninterrupted effort to furnish every Jewish home with a Jewish glow; to educate the Jewish leaders of tomorrow; to protect and preserve the Jewish faith and traditions.

TOURO COLLEGE

In 1990, I was employed by Touro College in New York as senior development officer. This involved working closely with Dr. Bernard Lander, president of the college, and his staff in seeking grants largely in support of Touro's overseas campuses.

MOSCOW COLLEGE

Upon the collapse of the Soviet Union in 1991, Touro promptly opened the Moscow Branch of its International School of Business and Management. The college-level curriculum dealt with the fundamentals of Western finance and accounting, taught by full-time visiting adjunct professors with simultaneous Russian translation through earphones. In 1991–1992, Touro substantially met the costs of the facility and launched a comprehensive fundraising effort with the cooperation of leading American legal and accounting firms in reaching out to selected clients for financial support.

I was involved in providing progress reports to the United States Agency for International Development, Offices of American Schools and Hospitals Abroad (USAID). Our basic emphasis was on the role of Touro's Moscow College as prototype for former Communist nations of ways in which their economies could shape an orderly transition to an American-type free market system. I advised the USAID of Touro's plan to launch thirty-day executive management seminars, starting in 1994, on the operations of emerging corporate-type ownerships and managements. By May 1992, the Moscow College had already held a number of two-day seminars with the cooperation of the New York law firm of Skadden, Arps.

In August 1992, we submitted a formal application to AID for a major grant for the construction and equipment needs of the Moscow College. This was in line with the Washington agency's interest in facilitating the shift to a market economy through management training and economics education projects. The application described the benefits of the proposed grant as follows:

Touro College has taken the initiative in establishing American business studies in Russia. Touro believes that the establishment of the Moscow College of International School of Business and Management is a vital step in the growing interchange between the U.S. and Russia for the benefit of citizens of both nations. The Touro program presents a remarkable opportunity for preparing emerging Russian business leaders for vital relationships with American trading and investment interests.

It was not until 1994 that the Moscow College received its first major grant. This came from the Eurasia Foundation in Washington, DC, which extended $160,000 for accounting certificate and degree programs. The foundation was funded by AID.

VLADIVOSTOK CENTER

In 1984, Touro created the Pacific Community Institute (PCI), initially based in Korea and Thailand and extended to Vladivostok, Russia, after 1991. The Far Eastern program looked to supervised student internships at American firms where practical experience would be gained. Planning for the institute looked to courses in computer science, the principles of accounting, economics analysis, and human behavior in a range of business organizations.

A preliminary approach for funding of the Vladivostok Center was a successful effort for the organization of a two-day conference in Jakarta, Indonesia by the Pacific Community Institute. The meeting reviewed Russia's changing role in relation to international efforts to limit Communist China's impact on small nations in Southeast Asia. The gathering analyzed the development of joint American and Asian guarantees of Southeast Asian neutrality and disarmament. The meeting also sought ways in which to develop attractive terms for business investments in Siberia as a common ground for Russo-Japanese-American participation. A basic challenge was the need to overcome the short supply of critical resources and products to fulfill population needs.

Lack of sufficient funding for a more comprehensive approach led to an effort to support the work of PCI's advisory council made up of the board of directors of the PCI, ambassadors, and governmental leaders. The advisory council looked to the eventual formation of a United States/Asia Parliamentarian Union. It was anticipated that Touro's Pacific Community Institute would serve as secretariat for the proposed Union.

In 1994, the Pacific Community Institute formally applied for a $700,000 grant from the United States Agency for International Development for support of the proposed Vladivostok Executive Management Center. The funding would be applied to three-month cycles of classes over two years, dealing with business practices and the principles of management, finance, and marketing.

The proposal stressed that an expanded Vladivostok campus would give the United States a sustained training presence in the eastern Siberian region. A special effort would be made to attract enrollees from university faculties who would have the opportunity to go back to their institutions to teach free market-related courses. Attendees would also include employees of government agencies responsible for the implementation of market reforms. The Vladivostok Center would also disseminate educational materials in the region, including case studies, media presentations, and software translations.

The proposal looked to the evaluation of the grant program through self-rating questionnaires for faculty and participants, a follow-up survey, and case studies of selected participants. The results of the evaluation would be applied to workshops in management training and market economics analysis.

Unfortunately, Touro College did not have sufficient clout to compete with similar applications from business schools of major American universities. Despite its pioneering role in bringing studies of American business practices to eastern Siberia, Touro's application to USAID was not funded, and the Vladivostok Executive Management Center did not survive.

Instead, Touro College was able to obtain a grant of $10,000 in 1994 for support of its Moscow-based program for the training of teachers at emerging Jewish schools in Russia. This grant, based on my proposal, supplemented support from the Jewish Agency for Israel for Russian Jewish student and teacher exchanges.

ISRAEL CAMPUS

Since 1986, Touro College has offered undergraduate courses and a master's degree in Jewish studies at its Yeshurun campus in Jerusalem. The program accommodated settlers from Russia after 1991, as well as optional one-year residencies for full-time students from Touro College in New York. In connection with the construction and naming of facilities at the campus, I drafted a proposal for the funding of an academic center, auditorium, library, and administrative facility at the Yeshurun campus.

This was the basis for an ongoing funding effort, starting with the raising of $15 million for construction in 1993–1996. Over time, major facilities were completed in Jerusalem, housing the Yeshurun College Graduate School. For support of Jewish studies at both the New York and Jerusalem campuses, I prepared another proposal for the establishment of family scholarship endowments for support of required courses in a range of Judaic studies. The College accommodates students majoring in these studies, and also offers a Master's degree in this field. Endowed scholarship was sought in each of these areas, as well as support of the undergraduate one-year option for study in Israel.

AMERICAN CAMPUSES

In 1994, I drafted a major 150-page proposal submitted to the California Council for Post-Secondary Education for accreditation of the Touro College of Osteopathic Medicine based in Vallejo, California, near San Francisco. Over time, the 44-acre campus also became the site of Touro's College of Health Sciences, College of Pharmacy, and the College of Education. These facilities became a major source of support for all Touro programs in New York, Jerusalem, and Moscow.

With a current enrollment of over 550 students, the College of Osteopathic Medicine maintains the values, philosophy, and practice of its discipline with a commitment to primary care and a holistic approach to patients in the best traditions of the Jewish heritage. Specifically, this approach applies manipulative techniques for correcting abnormalities thought to cause disease and inhibit recovery. Students are trained in a combination of subject areas, including anatomy, pathology, microbiology, pharmacology, and immunology applied to major functions of the body.

In 1994, I also participated in the drafting of a proposal that went to the United States Public Health Service for support of the Physician Assistant Program at Touro's School of Health Sciences in Dix Hills, New York. The proposal emphasized the training of minority and disadvantaged students for services in primary health care settings. The training covered nursing care, occupational therapy, and physical therapy for patients in medically underserved areas.

The Physician Assistant Program was presented in the successful funding application as a prototype, for replication nationally, to meet the demands of a wide-ranging healthcare program. In 1994, the program at Dix Hills had 79 students. Today, following the move to Manhattan, the School of Health Sciences has an enrollment of over 1,100. The 1994 funding application anticipated this increase, stressing the extension of health care through home-based, community-based, nursing home care to reach out to 40 million Americans who had no health insurance. Also, the effort to limit the hours of patient contact for resident doctors involved in postgraduate training looked to physicians' assistants to help meet the requirements of proper patient care. Touro's emphasis on the recruitment of minority and underprivileged students looked to service in their own communities.

The funding application stressed the need to evaluate the expanded training program to facilitate its replication. The application noted:

> Data on student self-ratings will be compared to faculty ratings to analyze changes from before and after rotations. The data will indicate perceptions of the effectiveness of primary care rotations based on the variety of patient contact, the adequacy of supervision provided, and the adequacy of facilities. The follow-up survey and case studies will track the impact of rotations at health care facilities and upon student development as Physician Assistants. The results of the evaluation will be published as a basis for its replication by other institutions.

My work at Touro College finished on this note.

Chapter Six

Development Consultant

BRITH HOUSE

In February 1996, I prepared a proposal and coordinated a fundraising effort for Brith House in Brooklyn to find and rehabilitate delinquent youths from Orthodox Jewish homes. These young people had rejected their religious and educational upbringing, run away, and resorted to criminal behavior. An intervention team from Brith House would bring these youths into a storefront therapeutic community to provide counseling, treatment and ongoing guidance.

The funding proposal describes an activity to provide individual psychotherapy, "rap sessions," and structured group encounter meetings. These would seek to bring participants to recognition of the need for change and for abiding by a "contract" for specific kinds of positive behavior. At the same time, the clinical intervention team would work with parents to bridge emotional gaps, and also visit with religious school administrators to facilitate reentry of such students into the classroom.

The proposed pilot project would deal with a severely underserviced need to assist many adolescents in crisis. Few established agencies were able to target this group, leading to financial burdens imposed on educational institutions and the criminal justice system. The absence of diagnostic measures was particularly evident in Orthodox Jewish religious schools that lacked the staff needed for psychological assessment. At the same time, Orthodox families were unable to cope with disaffected children in connection with belief and the practice of the tenets of traditional Judaism.

The proposal notes:

Orthodox Jewish adolescents are particularly vulnerable to alienation because:
a) family religious and cultural standards are so precise that deviation appears to

be particularly blatant; b) there are no culturally accepted alternatives for conduct and outlook in traditional households, resulting in total exclusion of some young people from a closely-knit society; and c) there is increasing disparity between secular and religious norms.

Elements in the proposed treatment program would seek to bring about behavioral changes through clinical interventions by the storefront facility, reinforced by a social system of group maintenance and intervention. These methods would be further refined at a planned residential facility for those who refused to return to their homes.

The therapeutic community concept would seek to draw individuals into a social framework that stressed interpersonal trust and concern in contrast to former dysfunctional family or street influences. In six-week cycles, young participants and staff clinicians would extend a participatory role to newcomers, constantly interacting with them and advancing them through the group structure. Pressures for conformity would also be matched by opportunities for personal gratification in abiding by the norms, including a sense of comradeship and participation in meaningful community activities. The goal of the program would be reintegration into the family, or alternatively to provide choices in lieu of return to excessively dysfunctional families. At the same time, the therapeutic community would also recognize the need to give the adolescent time away from the group in order to develop greater self-direction and assurance.

After each six-week cycle in the demonstration program, the clinical staff would continue to follow up on each individual to assure a level of long-term stability and socially acceptable conduct. Each participant would complete a personalized self-appraisal form, and would also be free to drop in at the project center to participate in "rap sessions" and meet with staff counselors. In some cases, there would be an opportunity to repeat a six-week cycle of participation. A staff family therapist would also continue to meet with family members at least once a month.

For replication of the project under other auspices, the proposal stressed an intensive evaluation of objectives. The $865,000 twelve-month project would be appraised on the basis of the following objectives:

A. Participants will develop greater self-awareness and self-control in handling personal problems and emotional difficulties through clinical, educational and recreational services reinforced by therapeutic community methods, in which group controls and influences are exercised.

B. Based on the effectiveness of treatment, participants will demonstrate greater capacity for adjustment and normal development within family structures, schools, and the community.

The external evaluator would compile and analyze data on selected/random sample participants two months after they leave the program. This would include client perception of the program and services rendered (including attitudes concerning staff and the effectiveness of services). Data for post-treatment behaviors would be obtained on current living arrangements, self-appraisal of life situations, ongoing contacts with the program and public and private agencies, educational and occupational activities, family and peer relationships, psychological signs (including anxiety, depression, and hostility), and/or involvement with law enforcement officials.

Outcome groups would be categorized by extent of participation in the program, age (at admission), and in accordance with the external investigator's appraisal of the success or marginal success of the program. These qualitative measures would be compared with data (complied by the Jewish Child Care Association's Brooklyn Preventative Services Project) for a random sampling of other dropout youth who did not undergo therapeutic community procedures.

The evaluation program, using rating scales, would also provide basic information on the utilization and effectiveness of peer interns as role models; the adaptation of clinical staff to therapeutic community procedures; and the extent to which these procedures can be replicated by non-pilot, ongoing programs in major areas of Orthodox Jewish and non-Jewish residence in New York and nationally.

My narrative now brings me to personal activities from 1987 to 2000. I established an acquaintance with Aaron Lansky, who was developing a repository for abandoned Yiddish books, which might otherwise be destroyed. He had established the National Yiddish Book Center in Amherst, Massachusetts, and sought the assistance of volunteers to visit homes with extensive Yiddish book holdings. Over a million volumes were deposited to the Amherst archive, where student volunteers sorted the books. As advisor for the project, I concentrated on the development of lists of Yiddish authors, as well as 450 libraries that would be interested in receiving selected volumes for their archives.

In September 1988, I attended the Bat Mitzvah ceremony (for 13-year-old Jewish girls) in Toronto of the daughter of George Leopold. Her grandfather, Aaron Leopold, was my mother's brother, the only one in her family, as I noted earlier, who survived the Nazi Holocaust. Aaron's other son, Harvey, also lives in Toronto, and the Bat Mitzvah was the occasion for a small family gathering with reminiscences.

The year 1988 marked my sale of acreage that my grandfather, Gershon Rappaport, had donated to me. This was my final parting from land near High

Falls, New York, that had been my grandfather's farm and the site of Lee-Ra Colony that my father had developed as a site for summer bungalows.

The following year was marked by our only overnight cruise on a windjammer. Naomi and I boarded the vessel in Camden, Maine, on August 30, 1989, for the trip to nearby Halifax. All our travels that followed were by auto and airliner. This was a basic departure from a family heritage, which had brought my parents to America by steamship.

In January 1990, we attended the performance of a Yiddish play by amateur members of the Folksbiene troupe. The manager several decades earlier had been Benjamin Levine, a businessman, who was the husband of my mother's cousin, Chane, who had come from Austria-Hungary. The players strove valiantly to preserve the classical Yiddish theater which had fallen victim to assimilation and vaudeville acts.

In 1996, my appointment book notes, I had several meetings with Jack Weprin, an attorney and real estate investor. Coming out of Brooklyn, Jack worked as a delivery boy for his father and finished law school at night school. His investments included several properties and a restaurant in Manhattan. It later became my task, as he lay dying of a heart ailment, to call his several children, who rushed to the Monticello Hospital in New York to witness his passing and mourn together.

BENSALEM RESCUE SQUAD

In June 1996, as campaign coordinator for the Bensalem Rescue Squad, Bensalem, Pennsylvania, I prepared a case presentation to raise $400,000 to expand its existing facility to accommodate more ambulances and supply rooms and crews for the Rescue Squad. At the June 26th meeting of the Campaign Advisory Council, Arnold D. Ody, chairman, and the Bensalem mayor, Joseph Di Giordano, outlined the need for a larger facility in the rapidly growing community and the mounting travel-related emergencies on the surrounding regional highways. The number of emergencies had grown to an unprecedented 5,000 each year, leading to a doubling of the Rescue Squad's budget requirements. Public funds were inadequate to sustain the squad, leading to the fundraising campaign.

The case presentation looked to the raising of ten challenge gifts in the corporate sector and from individuals to cover 40 percent of the campaign goal. A business and merchants committee was planned to promote special gatherings and broaden the campaign's outreach throughout the community.

During my tenure, I visited several businessmen, whose responses were generally quite negative. Unlike an appeal to foundations or representatives of large corporations, my requests for donations and pledges were met with certain hostility toward a paid fundraiser who did not live in the community. Generally, there was little awareness of the work of the rescue squad and a sense that the local hospital would continue to be able to handle all emergencies confronting residents. The Campaign Advisory Council became aware of these responses and was increasingly opposed to supporting a professional consultant. A planned campaign victory event did not take place, and an ongoing appeal concentrated on selected corporations and wealthy residents.

ASSAF HAROFEH MEDICAL CENTER

My work for the American friends of the Israeli hospital Assaf Harofeh began intermittently in 1995 and picked up two years later with my development of proposals for the purchase of equipment for the treatment of cancer patients. Located in central Israel, the medical center served a rapidly growing population extending in all directions from Ben Gurion Airport. A high proportion of bed patients admitted by Assaf Harofeh were factory workers with advanced cases of malignancy and bone disease who had failed to obtain regular diagnostic screening.

The Medical Center in 1997 embarked on an effort to encourage regular visits for preventive diagnostic imaging services. There was now a vital need for the acquisition of a Dual Head Multi-Purpose Integrated Gamma Camera for the early detection of cancer and bone disease, to be followed by treatment. Up to this point, over 290,000 outpatients were served annually, but without the full technological resources needed to accommodate more outpatient visits, the medical center looked to more staff visits to factories to facilitate needed diagnostic imaging services. The hospital was now in greater need of nuclear imaging technologies for the assessment of cancers. My proposal sought over $600,000 for the acquisition of the Gamma Camera.

In addition, the medical center looked to the expansion of its CAT Scan Unit as its main diagnostic facility for cancer detection and treatment. This would involve the installation of up-to-date Computerized Tomography Scanners at a cost of over $800,000 for each.

I drafted a third proposal to obtain funding for a $110,000 Flow Cytometer as a basic diagnostic tool for the detection of cancer cells in blood and other forms of leukemia and lymphoma. In 1997, Assaf Harofeh was one of a number of hospitals in Israel lacking a Flow Cytometer as a standard diagnostic tool for outpatient visits. This piece of equipment was also of vital importance for the development of innovative therapies for the treatment of cervical, ovarian, and prostate cancer.

Over time, fundraising on behalf of the vital equipment needs of the Assaf
Harofeh Medical Center was successful among Jewish-sponsored foundations in the United States. This reflects the attraction of American Jewish
philanthropy to the basic needs of the state of Israel, including its medical
requirements. An underlying element here is the need to present well-written
proposals for consideration by foundation boards. In my talks with young
people seeking careers, I continually stress the unlimited opportunities offered by voluntary organizations in need of ongoing funding. The ability
to write promising proposals, plus a record of successful fundraising, are a
certain guarantee of job placement in our society. I have repeatedly demonstrated this in the course of my many years as a development officer and
consultant.

NATIONAL FOUNDATION OF
TEACHING ENTREPRENEURSHIP

In 1997, I also drafted a cover letter for the organization which was training
inner-city youth for their placement, mentoring, and evaluation as salaried
apprentices at business firms. NFTE was now seeking to expand its mission
in lifting these young people out of the poverty cycle through the learning
and application of business skills, combined with the development of a strong
work ethic. My consultantship was on behalf of Steve Mariotti, president and
founder of NFTE.

On the basis of a ten-year record of achievement, NFTE was providing
entrepreneurial studies for over 3,000 minority youths in 1997 in thirteen municipalities, which included up to 100 hours of practical hands-on instruction.
Study materials were simplified presentations of curriculums at the MBA
level. Field trips to retail and service companies offered a vital introduction
to ways in which personal plans could be put to work in the business world.
NFTE staff and certified teachers offered ongoing mentoring for the apprentices, who also participated in entrepreneurial clubs and roundtables at local
NFTE headquarters. NFTE established national partnerships with Microsoft
and other leading corporations, which provided $15 million annually after
1990.

In 1997, I worked on a funding proposal which looked to the evaluation
of NFTE's program over an 18-month period for the appraisal of its performance and effectiveness. Criteria for evaluation would include the on-the-job
application of such skills and concepts as the writing of business correspondence, developing and making presentations, time management, budgeting,
negotiating, goal setting, and teamwork. The development and implementa-

tion of plans by the young people for launching their own businesses, on the basis of their apprenticeships, was to be a key part of the assessment of the funded project.

The application requested a grant of $100,000 as a vital demonstration of ways in which the teaching of entrepreneurship would be given practical application in the business world. The funded project would basically deal with the economic and social problems of America's low-income communities.

Since the 1980s, NFTE has reached more than 230,000 young people since its founding and currently has programs in twenty-two states and thirteen countries.

JORDAN RIVER VILLAGE

In 2003, I served as a short-term consultant to the Jordan River Village in Israel, established by Marilyn and Murray Grant. My service involved the inauguration of a fundraising effort in the United States to support the construction of facilities at the village to accommodate chronically ill Jewish and Arab children in a camp setting, at no cost to their parents.

The village would be patterned on the actor Paul Newman's Hole in the Wall Camp in Connecticut for young campers suffering from life-threatening diseases. In the year 2000, Mr. and Mrs. Grant launched the Jordan River Village on sixty-one acres of secluded, beautiful land high above the Sea of Galilee and promptly obtained the approval of the government of Israel and Paul Newman's association of camps for disabled young people. In the course of the development of the village, young campers from Israel were accommodated in Paul Newman's affiliated camps in the United States and Ireland.

I identified selected foundations with patterns of support for Israeli projects capable of making grants of $250,000 and over in support of a range of facilities to be built at the Jordan River Village. The goal was to raise $25 million to cover the cost of construction and help meet an annual budget of over $2.5 million. For these foundations, I provided Mr. and Mrs. Grant the names of individuals to be contacted and types of health services of special foundation interests. My correspondence with the Grants paid special attention to a short list of foundations in New York and Miami, for which I garnered information on their types of support, the size of gifts and items to be stressed in the submission of a funding proposal.

Construction at the Jordan River Village began in 2006, and the village will open in 2010.

I turn now to a brief chronology of the illness and death on September 27, 2007, of my wife, Naomi. Her treatment by a neurologist began in June 2002, and the beginning of loss of memory was detected in February 2005. Medications for memory loss did not halt its progression. Attendance at meetings of patients with memory loss was not constructive. At the same time, lung cancer was noted in the summer of 2007. There was continued deterioration throughout that year, until her passing. And so ended the great love of my life, and with it has come the need to carry on with the support of my children.

Chapter Seven

Israeli-Palestinian Relations

Beginning in 2006, largely under the sponsorship of the New York Council for the Humanities, I made over thirty lecture appearances at synagogues, community centers, and public high schools on the crisis in the Middle East. The following is the text that I prepared for these lectures, as of November 20, 2009.

This is a time of great stress for Israel, concerned with its own security, and facing demands for its disposal of protective lands. We are aware that Israel is a slim territory surrounded by a generally hostile Arab world. The Jewish state lives on the edge of a volcano. In what appears to be another Hundred Year War, the national Jewish home has become a fortress behind a barricade to protect its almost 6 million Jewish residents.

Yet through it all, Israel has developed a high-tech economy and intellectual oasis in the desert for the benefit also of its 1.5 million Arab citizens. I will trace Israel's remarkable development and defense up to current efforts to form a basis for a lasting peace in the spirit of Am Yisrael Chai (Israel lives).

The present crisis in the Middle East revolves around the West Bank, Gaza, Iran and Lebanon, and the world looks for recommendations on how the safety and national character of both Jews and Arabs may best be preserved.

BALFOUR DECLARATION

Today's critical events go back to the Balfour Declaration in 1917, issued during the British military expulsion of the Turks from Palestine, which looked to the establishment in Palestine of a national home for the Jewish people.

In a letter to Lord Rothschild on November 2, 1917, British Secretary for Foreign Affairs Arthur Balfour wrote, "His Majesty's Government view with favour the establishment in Palestine of a national home for the Jewish people, and will use their best endeavours to facilitate the achievement of this object, it being clearly understood that nothing will be done which may prejudice the civil and religious rights of existing non-Jewish communities in Palestine or the rights and political status enjoyed by Jews in any other country."

The American president Woodrow Wilson openly endorsed the Balfour Declaration in a letter to Rabbi Stephen Wise on August 31, 1918, writing, "I have watched with deep and sincere interest the reconstructive work which the Weizmann Commission has done in Palestine at the instance of the British Government, and I welcome an opportunity to express the satisfaction I have felt in the progress of the Zionist Movement in the United States and in the Allied countries since the declaration by Mr. Balfour on behalf of the British Government of Britain's approval of the establishment in Palestine of a national home for the Jewish people . . ."

Opposition to Balfour Declaration

On each anniversary of the Balfour Declaration, militant Arabs hold rallies demanding apology from Britain for the imperialistic establishment in Palestine of a homeland for the Jews. Britain was interested in developing a stable population in Palestine close to the Suez Canal, which Britain controlled since 1888. The Suez was passage to Britain's imperial jewel, India. Now Hamas leaders in Gaza assert that British Mandate Palestine is part of the Arab motherland, and are opposed to efforts for a two-state structure. Hamas is committed to the elimination of Israel.

For Hamas, the removal of Israel had been a higher priority than the establishment of a Palestinian state in the West Bank and Gaza, which Israel left in 2005. As a political party, Hamas in 2006 won a two-to-one majority of the representatives in the elected Palestinian Legislative Council. In June, 2007, in a civil war, Hamas defeated the moderate Fatah party, and gained full territorial control of the Gaza strip with over a million residents. This was a defeat, as well, for Israeli and American efforts at a two-state structure.

British Mandate Included Gaza and West Bank

Joint Israeli-American policy viewed the Balfour Declaration as the basis for recognition of Israel's territorial needs and the future of the West Bank.

Western nations also regarded the mandate as affirming the biblical roots of the Jews' moral, legal and historical claim to Palestine. Jews have lived in the Holy Land for over 3,000 years. King Faisal of Saudi Arabia supported the Declaration in 1919. When Britain assumed mandatory control over Palestine, with the approval of the League of Nations in 1922, the West Bank and Gaza were considered to be part of the proposed Jewish national home.

Israel has brought a new reality to the Jewish people, based on self-reliance and self-defense in opposition to Islamic extremism and a nuclear Iran. Israel has occupied and developed most of the territory of the British mandate, and stresses it must maintain its status as a Jewish state.

EARLY AMERICAN INVOLVEMENT

Major U.S. Party Platforms Supported Jewish Statehood

Contrary to the Balfour Declaration, in 1939 Britain issued the White Paper limiting Jewish immigration into Palestine, which led to a more direct American role regarding the future of the mandate. This established the foundations of today's joint American-Israeli defense and political strategy. In every presidential election the Republican and Democratic platforms supported the establishment of a democratic Jewish state in Palestine in accordance with the intent and purpose of the Balfour Declaration. It should be stressed that American support for Israel has long pre-dated extended pro-Zionist political activity in Washington. Active American involvement in the Middle East also goes back to the 1933 pact that the U.S. oil company Aramco signed with Saudi Arabia.

Labor Zionist Americans went to kibbutzim in Palestine in the 1930s to build the foundations of the Jewish state. A song at the time was: "Good-bye America/ Good-bye Yankee fashion/ We're off the Palestine/To heck with the Depression."

Major Powers Sought Division of Palestine After World War II

The Holocaust and the plight of Jewish refugees created an irrepressible demand for a free Palestine as a Jewish sanctuary. At the same time, the major powers began to consider the partition of the mandated area into Jewish and Arab sectors, while Jewish militants within Palestine resorted to force to get the British out. In 1947, the United Nations, like the League of Nations earlier, voted in support of the right of the Jews to a national home next to an

Arab state in Palestine. Arab militants blame the Holocaust for the emergence of Israel on land they say belongs to Palestinians, and fundamentalist Arabs chose war against the Jews. Arab terrorists began attacking Jews in December, 1947, prior to the proclamation of the State of Israel.

ISRAEL INDEPENDENCE

Jordan Controlled West Bank Following 1948 Invasion

When the British finally left in May, 1948, the State of Israel was proclaimed after six months of civil war. The Jewish population totalled 700,000. Arab militia commanders advised some 300,000 largely anti-Jewish Arab residents to temporarily evacuate Israel to facilitate their holy war against the new Jewish nation. An additional 100,000 Arabs left Israel in the wake of ongoing hostilities through 1948. The return of these Arab refugees would limit Israel's identity as a Jewish state.

The Arab catastrophe was the beginning of today's refugee problem. Arab governments have also created hundreds of thousands additional Muslim refugees evicted from Kuwait, Iraq, and Lebanon. Meanwhile, over 800,000 Jews were forced out of apartheid Arab lands in 1948, leaving behind real estate worth billions of dollars. Today, Jews no longer live in Islamic communities, except in Iran. Only a handful remain in Egypt, despite past Jewish contributions to major Egyptian institutions. Their economic losses far exceed the losses of Arab refugees from Israel.

The Jewish nation, under attack, had to accept the action of the United Nations in placing the West Bank under Jordanian control, which sought to wipe out all vestiges of the Jewish past.

Meanwhile, today, some Arab villages within Israel remain empty, despite the demands of refugees to return to them. President Bush had recommended that Israel arrange for monetary compensation for these lost homes in place of the right of return. There are now some 4 million actual or largely descendant Arab refugees in camps in five countries. Israel does not accept the principle of the "right of return" of these refugees to a Jewish nation, while the Palestinian Authority opposes their settlement in other countries. Little has been done to integrate the refugees in surrounding societies.

The plight of the Arab refugees greatly diminishes prospects for a two-state resolution of the current situation. Palestinians maintain that recognition of Israel as a Jewish state would compromise the right of return of Arab refugees. Direct negotiations between Israel and moderate Arab leaders might enable some of the refugees to settle in the West Bank. Israel ought also to be prepared to accept selected refugees who can be productive residents.

Israel Occupied West Bank and Gaza, 1967

Israel's armistice with Egypt in 1949 placed Gaza under Egyptian rule, which denied its citizenship for residents of the territory. Then Jerusalem became the official seat of the Israeli government. Egypt and Jordan did not set up a Palestinian state in the West Bank and Gaza between 1949 and 1967. In the1956 Suez War, Israel temporarily occupied the Sinai Peninsula, in coordination with Britain and France, and then withdrew under pressure from the United States.

Then in 1967, following Egypt's closure of the Gulf of Aqaba to Israeli ships and the removal of an UN peace-keeping force, Israel launched a pre-emptive attack against Egyptian and Syrian forces which were massed, with the assistance of the Soviet Union, to eliminate the Jewish state. The Six Day War resulted in Israel's occupation of Gaza, the West Bank, all of Jerusalem including the Temple Mount, the Golan Heights, and the Sinai Peninsula. If the Arabs had recognized Israel's borders in 1948, there would not have been a conflict in 1967.

The Yom Kippur War in 1973, launched by Egypt and Syria across the Suez Canal and the Golan Heights with over a million troops, brought American arms assistance to help preserve Israeli control. Egypt recognized Israel in 1979, and Jordan established diplomatic relations in 1994. This recognition should be emulated by other Arab nations. Egypt, Jordan and Saudi Arabia today support the peace process. Meanwhile, Arab militants are calling on Egypt to abandon its treaty with Israel.

Israel Returned Sinai to Egypt in 1982

Subsequent decades saw an Israeli willingness to give up territories which were not integral to its existence as a Jewish nation, combined with American support of the doctrine of "secure and defensible borders" for Israel. American policy traditionally recognized Israel's territorial needs in relation to the "natural growth" of its population. In exchange for a peace treaty, Israel under Menachem Begin returned the Sinai area to Egypt after evacuating Jewish settlements there in 1982.

Presidents Nixon and Carter played vital roles in advancing Israeli-Egyptian peace. In 2000, Israel also withdrew unilaterally from the security zone it had established in South Lebanon. This was followed by Hezbollah's arming of the border with rockets, counter to the UN's demand that the border be demilitarized.

OSLO ACCORDS

Accords Bar Non-Democratic Means on Future of the West Bank

The Oslo Accords, signed on the White House lawn in September, 1993 by Israel Prime Minister Yitzhak Rabin and PLO Chairman Yasser Arafat—in the presence of President Bill Clinton—was an effort to proceed on the transfer to the Palestinians of 95 percent of the West Bank and all of Gaza. In its Declaration of Principles, the Oslo Accords looked to peaceful coexistence, mutual security, and adherence to past agreements. Of special relevance today, the Accords barred the participation in Palestinian elections of parties seeking to implement their aims "by unlawful or non-democratic means." Yet, militants claim that the basic tenants of the Islamic faith deny recognition of the Jewish religion and nationality.

Under the Oslo Accords, the transition was to have begun with the disengagement of Israeli military and civil administration in Gaza and the Jericho area, to be replaced by the Palestinian police and the newly-formed Palestinian Authority. The Authority is a government organization, as distinguished from the Hamas and Fatah political parties. It was to be responsible for improvements in education, health, social welfare, and the rehabilitation of the refugees.

No Enforcement Mechanisms in Absence of a Palestinian State

The Oslo Accords looked to ongoing cooperation for water and electrical development, transportation and communication, and the establishment of a Palestinian Development Bank. But Oslo did not clearly spell out enforcement mechanisms, and there was no Palestinian state to act jointly with Israel—only the Palestinian Authority. Yet Oslo did establish diplomatic relations for Israel with nine non-Arab Muslim states and improved relations with Jordan. China and India recognized Israel. On the other hand, Oslo brought a sharp increase in anti-Israel violence, paving the way for the rise of Hamas. In 1999, Prime Minister Benjamin Netanyahu signed an agreement with Yasir Arafat for limited Israel land transfers in the West Bank.

Intifada, 2000–2004

However, talks stopped with the launching of the Palestinian armed Intifada in 2000, aided by Iran. The Intifada was also reflected in the 2001 attack on the World Trade Center in New York City. Yasir Arafat goal was to lower immigration and industrial growth in Israel. But President Bush refused to deal with Arafat, who rejected a two-state resolution. Bush approved Israel's armed intervention in the West Bank to clear it of pro-Arafat leaders.

This relates directly to the militant position today of the anti-Israel Hamas party in Gaza and the Hezbollah faction in southern Lebanon, which embrace an ideological militancy in support of the religious Islamic claim to all of Palestine. Hamas has the support of the President of Iran and militants in Lebanon who initiated raids into Israel, and hurled rockets against Haifa. Hezbollah has a strong youth recruitment movement, and is active in Egypt in the smuggling of weapons. Lebanon's new cabinet in November, 2009 has minority Hezbollah representation.

As in the year 2000, the Palestinian election in 2006 saw the intensification of a "culture of hatred" in Palestinian society Today, anti-Semitism has taken on the language of anti-Zionism and Israelphobia. Israel is accused of killing Palestinians to remove their vital organs for sale. In the past decade, Israel had to strengthen its border controls and roadblocks which are choking off economic development in the West Bank. Yet Israel must take preventive measures against terrorism. Meanwhile, the Palestinians have been unable to manage their internal affairs peacefully and competently, increasing widespread unemployment.

PALESTINIAN AUTHORITY

Absence of Strong Central Control to Negotiate the Future of the West Bank

With the succession in 2005 of Mahmoud Abbas as president of the reconstituted Palestinian Authority, there was opportunity to continue negotiations on the general basis of the Oslo Accords. Up to now, the Palestinian Authority has been officially committed to discuss coordination of disengagement with Israel, with a formal cease-fire and the elimination of weapons by most participants in the political process. But the Palestinian Authority has now ceased talks with Israel.

The surrender of weapons was resisted by Hamas and related right-wing elements. With the reluctant approval of President Bush, Mr. Abbas sought initially to bring Hamas into the political arena as a means of reducing its armed activity. Yet the Palestinian Authority was resisted by the militants, leading to further setbacks in efforts in peace talks.

TWO-STATE RESOLUTION

Road-Map

Mr. Abbas had looked to the Palestinian Authority and Israel's withdrawal from Gaza as part of a reciprocal Middle East peace plan for the West Bank, known as the Road-map. This elusive agenda, started in 2003 by the United States and several members of the European Union, was drawn despite unfulfilled preliminary arrangements for the establishment of a Palestinian state with provisional borders.

George Mitchell, appointed by President Barack Obama as special envoy in the Middle East, authored a 2001 report on terrorism that pointed the way to the Road-map.

The concept embodies the vision, with American support, of a democratic Palestinian nation, recognizing and living at peace with Israel, and with a productive economy. The Road-map looks to a halt in the expansion of Jewish settlement in the West Bank with the end of all violence against Israel. The Road-map opposes the destruction of Arab homes in East Jerusalem, and delineates benchmarks to assess progress and compliance.

Until 2009, a majority of Israeli citizens had believed in the goal of achieving peace through the transfer of Arab-populated territories now controlled by Israel. This called for a strong Palestinian Authority and the assurance of Israeli security. Former Prime Minister Ariel Sharon had agreed to limitations on new settlements, while permitting new construction within established blocs.

But militant Arabs interpret any Israel evacuation as a sign of weakness, which Israel must overcome. And the fate of former Israeli Prime Minister Ehud Olmert's "realignment plan" depends on current Prime Minister Netanyahu's and Arab interest in negotiation.

Israelis looked to a Palestinian state to absorb Arabs living in refugee camps in place of their settlement in Israel. At present, most Israelis reject negotiations on an independent Palestine until the development of a strong economic infrastructure in the area. At the same time, the United States is interested in recognition of Israel as a line of defense against anti-Western militants comparable to older Fascist and Communist threats.

Efforts for a two-state resolution followed 17 peace plans proposed from 1937 to 2003. Now President Barack Obama must confront Israel's demand to retain all of the land on its side of the security barrier under construction. At the same time, the proposed Palestinian state is divided into two separate parts. Netanyahu has come out for negotiations for a two-state resolution on the basis of a demilitarized Palestine and recognition of Israel as a Jewish state. Meanwhile Iran's nuclear development is a direct threat to Israel's security. I suggest that NATO might at this time step into the breach.

PROPOSED NATO INVOLVEMENT

I propose that NATO, the 26-member western military alliance that is already fighting the Taliban terrorists in Afghanistan and has a military training mission in Iraq, should advance a two-state resolution. NATO should over time expand its activities in the Middle East, and include Israel in its membership, as a vital part of the effort to counter Islamic extremism in countries bordering on Israel. I stress that Israel had applied for NATO membership in 1954. Israel is currently prepared to participate in NATO aerial exercises in the eastern Mediterranean.

NATO would in time place rapid-reaction mobile troops on the border of the proposed Palestinian nation. A NATO naval force can patrol Israeli's coastline. NATO would give Israel the assurance of security as a basis for further concessions in resumed negotiations with the Palestinians. President Obama continues to call for renewed negotiations for a two-state resolution.

In November 2007, our State Department appointed the retired NATO commander, General James L. Jones, to oversee security in Israeli-Palestinian relations.

A NATO presence, as trustee for the West Bank and Gaza, would be comparable to the UN peace-keeping force of 10,000 troops placed earlier on the Israeli-Lebanese border. NATO is embarked on missile defense training in the Middle East. NATO can help limit Iran's nuclear and long-range missile development, reduce arms smuggling across the Gaza border, and end arms shipments to Hezbollah in Lebanon. NATO can work to bring Lebanese recognition of Israel. There is at present no effective international armed force on the Lebanese border now controlled by Hezbollah, which maintains its own military equipment. The UN has called for the disarmament of Hezbollah.

An active NATO presence on Israel's borders would help the United States reduce our military involvement in Iraq, whose militants are supported by Iran. A cease-fire enforced by NATO would diminish pro-Hamas pressures by elements in Egypt, Saudi Arabia, and Jordan. A NATO presence would counteract Turkey's rift with Israel.

Without a NATO presence, the only way to stop the threat of rocket attacks is for Israel to seize parts of Gaza and southern Lebanon. This might be followed later by a long-term cease-fire, hopefully enforced by NATO. A NATO presence would be in line with joint U.S.-Israeli military exercises.

A NATO third force would recognize the shift of the center of gravity in the Arab world from the Mediterranean toward the Persian Gulf, with a disruptions in communications between two civilizations. This is reflected in the clash between Western democratic values and the spread of an Islamofascism obsessed over humiliations and with a thirst for revenge. The clash of civilizations is also reflected in sharp differences in learning and liberties. Islamic xenophobia denies the Jewish right to sovereignty, and profiles Jews as subject to attack. Between 1975 and 1991, the United Nations equated Zionism with racism.

A NATO presence would represent the West in the defense of liberty, democracy, the rule of law, and cultural freedom. Islam, on the other hand, believes that war is holy, and the killing of dissenters is permissible.

NATO can police the border between two civilizations, as it did in the clash between western democracy and Soviet Communism. Terrorists are operating on the Afghan-Pakistan border, and Israel is caught in the middle of the clash of civilizations. The threat against Israel is a threat against Western democratic values.

The clash of civilizations is reflected in Islamic polygamy, religious rule over individual rights, and a breakdown in academic, business, and scientific relations with the West. NATO's presence in the West Bank and Gaza will serve as a bulwark against Islamic fatalism over civilians caught in the crossfire and acceptance of martyrdom.

For Israel, reliance on NATO would be particularly vital following the United States' expected withdrawal of the bulk of our 140,000 soldiers from Iraq by the end of 2011. This withdrawal can only follow the establishment of civil peace and the disarming of militia groups in Iraq. At this time, America's presence in Iraq in resisting Al Qaeda influences is crucial for halting the further spread of terrorism in the Middle East. Yet, in Iraq, violence is escalating perpetrated by the Ba'ath Party. The United States presence in Iraq is demoralizing Islamic terrorists. Iraq should become a buffer state against Iran and the Arab world. Meanwhile, Obama has no firm policy on Afghanistan, and is seeking increased Pakistan resistance against terrorists in Afghanistan who might retreat into Pakistan to escape NATO forces.

President Bush had changed American policy from maintenance of the status quo to a policy of pro-democratic change. A NATO presence, with full American and European Union backing, will also bolster the Palestinian Authority in the West Bank. NATO can train a new Iraqi army. At this time, the American army is gaining the support of the nation's population against Iranian-supported militants. Our presence in Iraq will enforce the development of a federal Iraqi state as an example for other Middle East nations.

RISE OF HAMAS

The January 2006 election for the Palestinian Legislative Council saw a victory for the militant anti-Israel Hamas party, which claimed to be promoting domestic reform and the fight against corruption. Hamas used the ballot box as a means of coming to power, while pursuing anti-democratic terrorist objectives. Even as Israel left Gaza, Hamas is claiming it is resisting Israeli occupation of Palestinian sectors. In Gaza, the Arabs ransacked what Israeli had built up, and then turned around and blamed Israel for economic collapse. The militants attack Israeli self-defense as belligerency. Meanwhile, Hamas spreads its authority across all aspects of life in Gaza, demanding conformity with Islamic religious beliefs and practices.

The elimination of Hamas will help bring greater assurance of peace for Israel, which in 2006 opposed an armed Hamas' participation in the election as a violation of democratic principles. The election marked the failure of Palestinian Authority President Abbas' long-term goal of "One Authority, One Law, One Gun."

The 2006 election also saw the failure of the United States' effort to stop Hamas' militancy. Secretary of State Condoleezza Rice had argued that the participation of Hamas in the election was a necessary stage in the evolution of an orderly Palestinian political process.

BUSH ADMINISTRATION

Position on Jewish Settlement Blocs East of Jerusalem

At his meetings with Prime Minister Ariel Sharon in April, 2004 and a year later, President Bush affirmed that on the basis of both Israel's initial withdrawal from Gaza, the removal of Israeli troops from ceded parts of the West Bank, and a final accord with the Palestinians, the Jewish nation would reciprocally be able to retain contiguous settlement blocs east of Jerusalem.

Subsequently, the Bush Administration opposed the expansion of Jewish communities in the West Bank during any Israel-Palestinian negotiations. This reflects the U.S. position that unilateral territorial moves by Israel should not now be recognized as final borders. Underscoring the talks with former

Prime Minister Olmert is the strategic interest of the United States in peace in the Middle East.

United States as Intermediary in Division of the West Bank

In the legacy of American support of the Balfour Declaration, American policy has remained fundamentally friendly to the Jewish nation, and its right to defend itself. Meanwhile, the Palestinian Authority had been prepared to accept the United States as mediator because Washington is pushing for a two-state solution. It follows that a viable exchange of land for peace will have to based on the division of the West Bank, with NATO as a proposed intermediary.

In return for a continued Israeli presence in a part of the West Bank, in 2002 the first President Bush had extended to the Palestinians their own Balfour Declaration for the creation of a Palestinian nation living at peace with Israel. Unlike the Jews, however, the Palestinians did not take up the challenge, and in 2006 in Gaza voted for disorder. The second President Bush had also sharply criticized Syria and Iran for their support of anti-Israeli militants in Gaza and Lebanon. He sent more American troops into Afghanistan. Our Secretary of State Hillary Clinton now supports a provisional two-state structure based on support by the European Union and the United Nations.

To deal with Gaza and the West Bank, and as part of the American initiative in Israeli-Palestinian relations, Condoleezza Rice had dealt directly with the Saudi Arabian monarch and former Israeli Prime Minister Olmert in an effort to set up negotiation objectives. Initially, she put in place bi-weekly meetings between Olmert and Mahmoud Abbas of the Palestinian Authority, including meetings in the West Bank, dealing initially with the easing of the over 500 checkpoints and roadblocks to facilitate the movement of people and goods between Israel and the West Bank. The meetings had also dealt with the disarming of terrorists.

Annapolis Meeting

In July, 2007, President Bush called for a high-level regional peace conference in Annapolis, Maryland to begin building a Palestinian state based in the West Bank and barring Hamas. The conference was intended to prepare a framework for ongoing negotiations.

Annapolis represented a break in seven years of futile talks. The conference was supposed to consider broad principles for future enforcement on a step-by-step basis. In the interim, moderates could marginalize Hamas.

Israeli Prime Minister Olmert was not ready for specific proposals at the peace conference. Yet, he had discussed a broad agenda in ongoing meetings with Abbas, calling for mutual concessions. Olmert has now been indicted and brought to trial for fraud by the Jerusalem District Court for allegedly using contributions for personal travels when he was mayor of Jerusalem. Israel recognizes that the relationship with Washington is crucial. Abbas had called for discussion of borders, the status of East Jerusalem, the Arab refugees, the Jewish settlements in the West Bank, water and security. Delaying discussion of these issues, Israel's primary concerns are its security, particularly against Iran, and its preservation as a Jewish nation.

Decisions following the Annapolis peace conference can be based on a proposed NATO presence, as well as economic improvement in the lives of Palestinians. Following Annapolis, over $7 billion was pledged by 80 nations over three years to fund economic development in the West Bank and to strengthen Israel security.

The United States looked to direct ongoing talks by Israel and the Palestinian Authority. At the same time, Israel will not negotiate directly with Hamas which refuses to recognize Israel. Yet we must work with the Arabs to resolve differences on the initial basis of Saudi Arabian and Syrian attendance at the Annapolis meeting. Backing up Olmert-Abbas meetings were teams of negotiators on civil, economic, and judicial issues.

Meanwhile, Egypt had brokered a tenuous truce relating to Gaza only, while Israel demanded assurances against rockets and the smuggling of weapons. Israel must have the ability to conduct military operations to stop assaults against the Jewish nation and legal Jewish settlements in the West Bank. Moderate Arabs must face down the Arab radicals to bring about a moderate secular solution in place of a no-win military option. There must be a general renunciation of violence in the Middle East, assuring Israel of security. Egypt should have an active role in preventing the re-arming of Hamas and in the strengthening of Fatah.

LEGAL JEWISH SETTLEMENTS IN THE WEST BANK

Negotiations between Israel and the Palestinians in the West Bank must deal with a growing population of over 300,000 Jewish residents in 122 Israeli-approved West Bank population blocs. Some 60 percent of the West Bank is under full Israeli control in both legal and unauthorized settlements. The current Palestinian-Arab population here is 2.4 million. Almost 60,000 housing units were built by Israel in the West Bank in the past 40 years. The government has authorized the building of 445 new houses and the completion of work on 3,000 houses prior to a 6–9 month freeze on new construction in anticipation of renewed peace talks with the Palestinians.

The Israeli government is interested in retaining control over these settlement blocs, some of them stretching several miles, which were part of the original British mandate as recognized by the former League of Nations and the United Nations. The legal settlements were not reduced by the Oslo Accords.

Pending renewed peace talks, President Obama wants limited expansion of construction in the settlements. Netanyahu would stop any new settlements, while seeking construction in established settlements to accommodate their "natural growth." At the same time, Netanyahu has approved the building of new settlements in the Jordan Valley to help monitor local activities.

There should be limitations on the expansion of legal Jewish settlements. At the same time, construction ought to continue inside settlements that Israel intends to keep in a future peace deal. Israel has issued permits for a number of legal settlements east of the security fence, and has been developing new housing east of Jerusalem.

The Israeli fence is enclosing most of the legal settlements. There have been no organized terrorist attacks behind the wall in the past two years, even in Arab towns inside Israel. But the building of the fence has led to clashes with displaced Arabs residents. Israel has killed Palestinian gunmen seeking to demolish sections of the fence. Other Israelis are accused of killing Palestinians in the West Bank. Some of the authorized settlement blocs control territories outside their official jurisdictions. The Israeli Supreme Court has ruled that a number of West Bank Arab villages should not be separated from surrounding farmlands.

Israeli Annexation of Western/Central West Bank

I am suggesting that in view of the original recognition of the West Bank by the Balfour Declaration as part of the future Jewish national home, the western/central areas of the West Bank with established Jewish settlements extending east and north of Jerusalem, ought to remain interconnected parts of Israel.

This area serves as a vital direct north-south route for Israel's military forces. Israel is also building a road connecting Jerusalem with the Jewish settlements, as well as a second road linking the Palestinian areas around Bethlehem and Jericho. The Arab-populated section of East Jerusalem might at this time become the administrative center for the proposed Palestinian state while remaining under Israeli control.

Greater Jerusalem in Exchange for Evacuation of Gaza

The Gaza evacuation by Israel should be the basis for the reciprocal annexation by Israel of Jewish settlements directly east of Jerusalem. This Greater Jerusalem, opposed by Hamas, would have to be recognized by Palestinians in a final peace agreement with Israel.

In view of its historical legacy and ongoing defense of its territorial integrity, Israel ought to retain East Jerusalem with 200,000 Jews, which it formally annexed after 1967. Israel's claim to Jerusalem goes back to King David, who made it capital of his kingdom. Today, the Jewish cemetery on the Mount of Olives is regarded as a holy site in the East Jerusalem sector. In 1995, the United States Congress passed the Jerusalem Embassy Act recognizing Jerusalem as the capital of Israel.

Currently, Jerusalem's mayor unfortunately seeks to demolish numerous Arab residencies to create a national park dedicated to biblical history, outside the walled Old City. At the same time, Arabs have been throwing stones at Jews visiting the Temple Mount compound. Hamas denies that all of Jerusalem can be claimed by the Zionists, while Israel looks to new housing in disputed parts of Jerusalem.

Building Palestinian Institutions

Most Israelis support the creation of a peaceful Palestinian state. Most of the northern West Bank, as well as Bethlehem and Jericho in the middle and south, should be joined as a contiguous Palestinian state with a connecting highway. In lieu of fixed boundaries at this time for the formative Palestinian nation, American policy emphasizes the building of viable institutions, the development of a police force, and the halt of Palestinian attacks. The Palestinian Authority is developing an administrative structure in the Bilin sector in the West Bank as a model for Palestinian statehood. Currently, Islamic militants interpret any Israeli willingness to give up land as a sign of weakness. Yet Israel's neighbors have up to now turned their part of the Land of Milk and Honey into a desert.

UNAUTHORIZED JEWISH SETTLEMENTS

Israeli law requires that West Bank Jewish settlements be built on state-controlled land. Over one hundred unauthorized Jewish settlements, surrounded by a majority of non-Jewish residents, were set up since 1967 without government approval or on seized Palestinian-owned land and houses. I stress that all land acquisitions by Israelis in the West Bank must be approved by the Ministry of Defense. At this time, new construction continues in at least twelve illegal settlements in the West Bank, without approval by the Defense Ministry.

The evacuation of most of these settlements, built after March, 2001 and which received unauthorized public funds, will impact on some 100,000 Jews living outside of Israel's 500 mile barrier under construction. Some of these residents are in favor of moving into Israel, with compensation. Other illegal outposts are building new houses, and there have been clashes with Palestinian neighbors. Palestinians in these sectors are being relegated to an underclass, and are subject to ongoing abuse. Israel has been demolishing some illegal structures in the West Bank. Jewish evacuations would advance a two-state resolution in Israeli-Palestinian relations. The evacuation would also strengthen Israel's democratic form of government.

However, Israeli Prime Minister Benjamin Netanyahu will not disband most of these settlements. On the other hand, the Obama Administration is opposed to their expansion in an effort to improve United States relations with the Muslim world. Obama advises that additional settlement building does not contribute to Israel's security. Israel's defense minister Ehud Barak is having a series of meetings with George Mitchell, and agreed to a temporary halt to new settlement construction while completing current building. Most Israelis view Obama as more pro-Palestinian than pro-Israeli, and maintain he has failed to move Arab governments to normalization of relations with Israel.

In June, 2005, Israel's Ministry of Housing stopped construction at seventy proposed new settlement sites in the West Bank, and has promised to dismantle twenty-four outposts. It follows that the Israeli government must halt the diversion of public funds for the building of roads to hilltop West Bank settlements. These outposts are not part of Israel's infrastructure, and do not meet the test of "defensible borders." In return for a temporary freeze on new buildings in settlements, Israel seeks reciprocal steps by the Arab world to ensure Israeli security.

Meanwhile, other legal Jewish settlements in less than ten percent of the West Bank will continue with the construction of facilities. Israel will not freeze growth in established settlements until the very end of any Road-map negotiations. At the same time, Israel must stop abuses against Palestinians living in areas of expanded Jewish settlement, including attacks against Arabs over disputed grazing lands and olive groves.

Resettlement Versus Anti-Disengagement Activity

In the interests of peace, ideological views must not outweigh the rule of law. Indeed, Israel has demonstrated that it is prepared to detain any of its own citizens resisting resettlement or contemplating intrusions or attacks upon Muslim sites. Yet some fifty-thousand Orthodox Jews live deep in the West Bank, and an equal number live in established settlements around Jerusalem.

Israeli militants have organized marches and other disruptions in the West Bank, blocking highways and intersections. Rather than engage in combat against Israeli soldiers, the Orthodox have burned Palestinian fields to frighten the farmers. Orthodox Jews have also caused rioting against Arabs during religious high holy days. The ultra-Orthodox do not recognize the Israeli government, saying that only the Messiah can bring Jewish statehood.

Orthodox Jews, escorted by Israeli soldiers, regularly visit Joseph's tomb in Nablus, a Palestinian city in the West Bank. This follows from the Oslo Accords, which granted Jews free access to Jewish holy sites in the West Bank. Meanwhile, in Hebron, Fatah security forces work with the Israeli security forces to keep order.

State Versus Rabbinical Authority

These activities raise the fundamental issue of rabbinic versus state authority, involving a clash between a messianic vision for a Greater Israel and the secular Medinat Yisrael. Two former Chief Rabbis have reiterated their call to soldiers to refuse orders related to the uprooting of unauthorized Jewish settlements. Religious Zionists regard Israel's invasion of Gaza in December, 2008 as part of a holy war. Ultra-Orthodox Jews oppose the movement of buses and cars in East Jerusalem on the Sabbath.

These religious Zionists, who bring the threat of ongoing cleavage between religious and secular elements, are a major challenge to Israel's security services. Orthodox resistance against Israel is ideological and not battle-related. The resolution of these differences needs to be based on a dialogue between religious and secular views based on a shared Jewish culture.

ARABS IN ISRAEL

Arab Citizens of Israel as Force for Two-State Resolution

In addition to the abandonment of illegal settlements in the West Bank, Israel should cultivate its own Arab citizens to work for peace. The peace effort could be advanced by 1.5 million Arabs who already live in Israel. This compares with a Jewish population of six million. And Israeli is obligated by the legacy of the Balfour Declaration to protect the citizenship and religious rights of non-Jewish communities which are overwhelmingly peaceful.

Israel's Declaration of Independence in 1948 also promised full civil rights for Arabs. Arabic is also an official language in Israel.

However, the Israeli right-wing regards them as a fifth-column, and points to a recent killing of eight seminary students by a free-moving Palestinian from East Jerusalem. In the summer of 2008, two Palestinian drivers of construction vehicles went on deadly rampages through central Jerusalem. Israeli militants note that Muslims in Israel were sympathetic toward Palestinians in Gaza during the 2009 Israeli invasion.

The Israeli cabinet has approved the inclusion of a Muslim member, and there are eleven Arabs in the Israeli parliament. The Druze and Bedouin communities participate in Israeli military service, and many Arabs attend local colleges.

Yet, Arab citizens of Israel still have certain legal disabilities. Arabs living in Jerusalem can vote in municipal elections, but not in national elections. Unfortunately, Israel's Central Elections Committee barred the two main Arab parties from running in the February 10, 2009 national election. Israel must deal with the accusation that it is becoming an apartheid state. Compare this with Arabian apartheid policies against Jews who no longer live in Arab countries, except in Iran.

Most Arabs living in Israel have family ties with Arabs in Gaza, the West Bank, and Lebanon, which can advance prospects for peace. There are over 100,000 aliens who left Arab lands to live and work in Israel, and maintain contacts with Palestinians. Daily, Arabs enter Israel for employment with legal protections, and could be a force for reconciliation. Israel is also encouraging Arabs to do business with Jews in Jenin in the northern West Bank.

The Jewish presence in the Middle East is an ongoing opportunity for Arab modernization and democratic development. Arab exposure to Western ideals in Israel on the sanctity of life would help overcome the Islamic glorification of death. There is an Israeli-based movement working for equal rights for Palestinians in the West Bank. In dealing with suicide bombers, let all Arabs become aware of Golda Meir's statement: "We can perhaps someday forgive you for killing our children, but we cannot forgive you for making us kill your children."

FUTURE OF GAZA

Evacuation Temporarily Improved Israel's Relations with Muslim States

The evacuation of eight-thousand Jewish settlers from Gaza in 2005, following Israel's earlier withdrawal from southern Lebanon, brought passing praise from a dozen Arab and Muslim nations. The evacuation at least separated terrorists from other Palestinians, and led the United States and Israel to resume their strategic dialogue on Middle East affairs. Some of Israel's neighbors have joined the European Union in denouncing terrorism and called for the recognition of Israel.

Economic Development in Gaza and the West Bank

Over the next ten years economic growth can be promoted through water treatment projects, the development of a seaport, and the modernization of the Gaza's airport with a cargo terminal. The construction of a rail line and road passages can link Gaza and the West Bank. Gaza needs industrial facilities, housing, hotel and greenhouse construction. Yet, until today, the rebuilding of Gaza has hardly begun. Seventy thousand workers in the private sector have lost their jobs, and 85 percent of its factories are shut down or operating at minimal capacity. Eighty percent of Gaza's population receives some form of assistance. The digging of over a thousand tunnels between Egypt and Gaza has developed a flourishing trade employing thousands of Palestinians.

Easing of Border Crossings into Israel Following End of Terrorism

The central role of the United States in Middle East negotiations was marked by Washington's initiative in bringing about the November, 2005 Palestinian-Israeli agreement on the border crossings between Gaza and Egypt. In response to terrorism, Israel had severely reduced movement across this dividing line, denying shipments into Gaza of materials pledged by numerous governments. The United States brought about an agreement on the automation of customs checkpoints to facilitate movement.

But Palestinian militants have destroyed some of this equipment, and Hamas fugitives have moved from Egypt into Gaza. The Palestinian Authority has been unable to establish adequate controls over border crossings, and failed to stop the digging of terrorist tunnels into Egypt for the smuggling of weapons.

Following the completion of Israel's protective barrier, the easing of border crossings and road blocks would give residents and businesses in Gaza greater access to jobs and markets in Israel and Egypt. At this time, Israel is keeping the border crossings and naval blockade of Gaza under tight control as long as Palestinian missiles remain a threat. There are other checkpoints down the middle of the West Bank, which Israel is prepared to ease, along with the elimination of many military surveillance posts in a test of Road-map goals.

Currently, Israel is seeking to establish a series of border crossings to be built adjacent to southern Gaza. The United States has negotiated the immediate deployment of European Union inspectors to monitor Palestinian control of the current Rafah and Karni crossings on the Egyptian-Gaza border leading to Israel. Hamas has accepted the presence of European inspectors to reopen the Rafah crossing which was closed by Israel in response to the threat of terrorism. Israel has also planned the construction of terminals along the West Bank border at a cost of $500 million.

CURRENT CONFLICT

Netanyahu Coalition

At this time, Israel must continue to act against Hamas militancy in Gaza, aided by Iran. The Netanyahu government firmly believes that security for Israel can follow only with the crushing of Islamic assailants. In the long term, the Prime Minister would support U.S. policy goals for the emergence of a peaceful Palestinian state. He opposes Hezbollah's inclusion in the Lebanese government.

At this time, the Netanyahu coalition points to the failure of the centrist parties to stop the smuggling of weapons into Gaza, the failure to defeat Hamas and Hezbollah, and ongoing Fatah's ties to Hezbollah, Syria, and Iran. Netanyahu of the Likud Party was able to build a right-wing coalition with the Shas Party, the Labor Party, and the Avigdor Lieberman faction to take over the government.

Likud Party members reject any territorial compromise with Palestinians, while Netanyahu supports an economic peace with the Palestinians pending any political negotiations. He supports Israeli construction in all parts of Jerusalem. In regard to Jewish holy sites, Netanyahu will not divide Jerusalem, and demands recognition of Israel as a Jewish state. He opposes the dismantling of most Jewish settlements in the West Bank, and supports housing construction within established settlements to accommodate their natural growth. He would complete three thousand units of new housing, and then freeze new construction. He advised Obama he opposes new Jewish settlements in the West Bank. He said the Temple Mount should remain with Israel, and looks to Egypt and Saudi Arabia to help stop rocket attacks.

Netanyahu's first objective is to stop Iranian nuclear development. He looks ultimately to a new Palestinian state, with limited self-rule, and with Israel in control of the borders and airspace to secure Israel militarily. Foreign Minister Lieberman stresses economy, security, and the defeat of Iran before any political solutions with the Arabs are pursued.

HAMAS TERRORISM

No Territorial Concessions Under Threat of Terrorism

In regard to the two-state resolution of current Israeli-Palestinian differences, Israel remains united in opposition to any territorial concessions in the West Bank that would compromise Israeli security. There is a general view that the West Bank must not become the site of rocket assaults against central Israel. To the north, Hezbollah would be able to hurl rockets against Tel-Aviv. At the same time, in June, 2009, pro-democracy candidates in Lebanon won a parliamentary majority backed by Western nations.

Continued Military Action

Israel continues to hold some eight thousand Fatah and Hamas convicts, most of whom have killed or were planning to kill Israelis. Egypt is negotiating the release of some Palestinian prisoners in exchange for a captive Israeli soldier. In October, 2009, Israel released twenty Palestinian women prisoners in exchange for proof that Gilad Shalit was alive as a Hamas captive. Shalit appeared in a video very much alive.

In the summer and fall of 2006 until today, there have been assaults by Israelis, Palestinians, and Lebanese. There have been killing by Israel of Arabs placing explosives at the security fence. Following Israel's evacuation of Gaza, Palestinians had fired rockets into Israel, some reaching major population areas. This reflects the failure of Israel's unilateral evacuation, and points to the need for mutual concessions. Arab dictatorships need the conflict to stay in power.

Following the Hamas victory in Gaza in the January, 2006 elections, Israel continues to plan a buffer zone on its border with Gaza. The Jewish state is also building an anti-missile system capable of knocking out short and long-range rockets. The only way to ensure Israel's security is for the elimination of terrorist enclaves on its borders, which might be accomplished by NATO.

Rocket Attacks

Israel cannot be expected to remain passive against the threat of rocket launchings. In September, 2009, two rockets hit Israel from southern Lebanon. In November, 2009, Hamas test-fired a rocket that flew thirty-seven miles into the sea, putting Tel Aviv within range. Hamas had fired missiles and mortars into Israel in early 2009. Yet, in the fall of 2009, this rocket-firing has ceased.

Israel's position is that if the Palestinian Authority is unable to stop terrorism from striking the Jewish nation, then Israel's Defense Forces will have to do it. Israeli incursions into Gaza had continued after the Annapolis meeting. In January, 2009, Israel's air force attacked a truck convoy in the Sudan carrying arms. In September, 2009, two rockets were launched from southern Lebanon against Israel. To make matters worse, Israel does not have diplomatic relations with Lebanon.

Since 2004, sixteen Israelis were killed by rockets. Until the Egyptian-brokered truce in June, 2008, the town of Sderot was hit by some two thousand rockets. The town has become a symbol of Israel's resistance to terrorism. Up to now, over thousands of rockets, missiles, and mortars have hit Israel, some reaching the coastal city of Ashdod. Israel looks to the Palestinian Authority to develop the necessary strength to crush the terrorist organizations, and is even sending weapons to Palestinian security forces. The rockets are in violation of the most basic norms of international law, and Israel is justified in its bombing of smuggling tunnels along Gaza's border with Egypt. Israel has also hit vehicles in Gaza carrying men suspected of launching rockets.

At the same time, efforts by the Palestinian Authority to confiscate weapons carried by Hamas members have led to kidnappings and gun battles between Muslims. Palestinians are caught between raids by Israeli troops and internecine conflict. A culture of violence and double-talk has replaced the language of brotherhood in Islamic society, and Palestinians have become prisoners in their own neighborhoods. Israel has sealed houses that had been occupied by Palestinian gunmen. Some applicants to foreign universities are unable to leave Gaza.

Every effort must be made to end the view in the Muslim world, including school curriculums, that violence is a legitimate means for resolving disputes. Schools must deny that suicide bombers will achieve martyrdom. A two-state resolution would be achieved only when Palestinians realize they cannot destroy Israel. Arabs must recognize that the Islamic religion can accept the existence of Israel. Meanwhile, there is a fundamental clash between Islam and the West. Arab moderates are overwhelmed by extremists who represent violence and repression. Young Arab students demonstrate certain discontent and concern.

Hamas as Terrorist Organization

The Obama Administration regards Hamas as a terrorist organization, and has not blocked Israel's efforts to end the Hamas government. On the other hand, Hamas believes that worsening conditions in Gaza will strengthen its rule and bring more aid from Europe and the Islamic world. Hamas maintains that Islamic contacts with Israel are contrary to religious beliefs, and that the Holy Land belongs to Islam. Arab militants want total victory with no compromise.

Yet, Hamas is in lengthy negotiation with Israel for the release of the captive soldier Gilad Shalit in exchange for the release from Israeli prisons of selected terrorists, including Marwan Barghouti, who can be a potential heir to Mahmoud Abbas as president of the Palestinian Authority. As of November, 2009, there has been no agreement.

Hamas defends its possession of weapons so long as Israel, as it says, continues its occupation of Palestine. Hamas' leadership war room was located in the basement of Gaza's leading hospital, and rockets have been stored in mosques and schools. Hamas' support of a private militia and Lebanon's accommodation of Hezbollah have made a sham of democratic values.

For Hamas, as part of its anti-Western outlook, the return to pre-1967 borders and the dismantling of all Jewish settlements in the West Bank must proceed any negotiations for a long-term cease-fire. Hamas does not currently recognize any agreements between Israel and the Palestinian Authority, and will not jail militants. Following Israel's invasion of Gaza in January, 2009 Hamas regained control of remaining Gaza tunnels.

Hamas is expanding its 20,000 military force. Long-range rockets are being smuggled into Gaza by tunnel and by sea. These rockets are now capable of hitting Beersheba and Ashdod. The tunnels also bring in computers, gasoline and clothing to supplement the daily arrival of a hundred truckloads of food and medicines from Israel, financed by the Europian Union.

Fatah and Hamas have been unable to agree on a unity government, while Fatah calls for new elections in Gaza. This points to the significance of the proposed NATO guard on the Israeli-Palestnian border to halt the expansion of terrorism with Iranian assistance. Fatah is unable to exercise governmental authority in the West Bank. which remains dependent on Israel for security and commerce.

Egyptian efforts to develop negotiations between Fatah and Hamas have led to futile talks between the two factions in Cairo. Yet, in September, 2009, Hamas indicated it would agree to a reconciliation with Fatah following Egypt's reopening of the Rafah border crossing between Sinai and Gaza. But Egypt's role has continued to decline, due to Syrian influence.

THE EMERGENCE OF IRAN

In October, 2005, Iran's president Mahmoud Ahmadinejad declared that whoever recognizes the Zionist regime acknowledges "the surrender and defeat of the Islamic world." He has repeated his demand for the elimination of Israel, and has helped arm militants in Gaza and Lebanon with thousands of rockets. He claims that Hezbollah has shattered the myth of Israel's invincibility. Addressing the UN General Assembly, the Iranian president described the Zionists as murderers and invaders. He repeated his verbal attacks at the UN Geneva conference on racism in April, 2009, and denied the extent of the Holocaust. He selected as Defense Minister an individual accused of perpetrating the 1994 bombing of the Jewish center in Buenos Aires, Argentina.

Iran is in the throes of massive protests against the declared results of the 2009 presidential election. While Obama favors continued talks with the regime, Israel looks to the mass demonstrations as beneficial for its relations with Arab governments.

Nuclear Development

Since 2002, Iran has been building nuclear facilities in a number of sites. Iran has also produced long-range missiles capable of reaching Israel. Most Arab governments have remained silent over the nuclear developments in Iran. At the same time, the UN Security Council is reviewing ways of deterring Iran from developing nuclear weapons, and has called for sanctions against the import of materials used for nuclear processing. The Security Council, which refused membership for Iran, has called for an international effort to monitor Iranian nuclear development. But Iran is concealing a number of atomic facilities it is building in the event some of its established sites are bombed.

Netanyahu indicated he would negotiate with the Palestinians only if the West stops Iran's work on a nuclear bomb. Of all issues, Iran is the chief concern of Israel. Israel maintains the West should stop nuclear development in North Korea as a basis for dealing with Iran. Meanwhile, President Obama said two-state negotiations would strengthen the international effort to stop Iranian nuclear development, and continues to affirm that Iranian nuclear development is unacceptable. He is developing plans for more stringent economic sanctions against Iran with the participation of China. Netanyahu supports a proposal of the European Union and Russia to have Iran ship enriched uranium to the West to be processed for non-military use, or else face sanctions. Iran opposes this plan.

In response, Iran's president has threatened to stop cooperating with the UN's International Atomic Energy Agency. Iran may be tapping into Pakistani sources on nuclear bomb development, and is reaching into the nuclear black market. In 2010, Iran will have the capacity to produce at least one nuclear bomb.

The United States is enforcing sanctions against companies aiding Iranian nuclear research, while President Obama is reaching out to the religious mullahs to stop the development of a nuclear bomb. In September, 2009, Iran agreed to have talks with Obama, which have not taken place for thirty years. Sanctions against Iran should be joined with a threat to use force against its nuclear sites. Meanwhile, Iran continues to send arms to Hamas and Hezbollah in violation of UN Security Council resolutions.

The European Union, supported by Russia, is also preparing to set up economic sanctions against Iran, but the threat of sanctions has not stopped Iranian nuclear development. Iran has threatened retaliation, which may include an effort to turn West European Muslim communities against national political leaders. Iran has also staged naval and military maneuvers in the Persian Gulf through which major oil shipments pass. The American response was to send a naval strike force into the Persian Gulf.

President Bush had affirmed that the United States, as guardian of democratic values in the Middle East, would defend Israel militarily against Iran if it threatens to launch missiles with nuclear warheads. The United States deployed an advanced radar system to the Negev desert. At the same time, there must be a threat of international military intervention to stop Iranian nuclear development. Thus far, the only response from the Iranian president has been that he would be interested in talks with President Obama. If diplomatic efforts fail, an American military strike against Iran is feasible and credible.

Meanwhile, Israeli Prime Minister Netanyahu has called for international action against Iran to stop its nuclear development. Israel had attacked nuclear developments in Iraq in 1981 and in Syria in 2007. An Israeli attack on Iranian nuclear facilities would bring rocket firing against Israel from Iran, Gaza, and southern Lebanon. Russia has launched a satellite to enable Israel to monitor Iran's nuclear activities. Russia is also considering the termination of a contract to deliver long-range missiles to Iran. Egypt and Jordan have severed diplomatic relations with Iran. It is rumored that in September, 2009, Netanyahu went to Moscow to express concern over the possible sale of anti-aircraft missiles to Iran.

Israel demands the cessation of enrichment of nuclear fuel in Iran which would lead to the development of a nuclear bomb. As a final alternative, the United States and Israel can launch non-piloted drones to attack Iranian nuclear sites. America has used these drones to attack militants in Pakistan and Afghanistan.

In response, Iran has financed control towers in southern Lebanon to identify targets in northern Israel in the event of a military confrontation over its nuclear program. Meanwhile, the United States and Israel are moving to a defense arrangement to counter international Islamic terrorism. The United States' presence in Iraq remains a deterrent to Iran's growing influence.

ISRAEL'S DILEMMA

The emergence of Iran has had a deep impact on Israel, and has led to further delays in talks with the Palestinians. Basically, Israel is committed to its own preservation as a unified democratic state with secure borders and a strong Jewish identity. Israel's population and leadership are now torn by a Jewish heritage of adherence to justice and morality as opposed to current demands for military security. This dichotomy is reflected in the sealing of the crossing points into Gaza, which have drastically reduced the amount of goods entering the territory. Increasingly, young American Jews have been critical of Israel for the suffering of Palestinian Arabs as contrary to Jewish tradition. Yet, Israeli's military have acted honorably toward the Palestinians.

Israel's dilemma was reflected in December-January, 1908–09 when the nation undertook a major military offensive into Gaza to stop rocket firings by militant Moslems. Over a thousand non-uniformed militants were killed. Israel demands that international law should protect attacks against terrorists.

A UN investigation in 2009 condemned Israel's treatment of civilians before and during its attack on Gaza, and also criticized Hamas for using civilians as shields. The report failed to distinguish between aggression and the right of self-defense. The UN report placed Israel on the same level as Hamas. The UN did not write a report on Hamas' firing of rockets.

Meanwhile, rockets continue to be smuggled into Gaza across the Sinai Peninsula and by tunnels from Egypt. Israel had hoped that, in the long term, the two-state resolution would greatly diminish Palestinian holy war sentiments. Israel looked to a non-militarized Palestinian state to promote ongoing negotiations on final borders and the status of West Bank settlements.

Currently, however, any discussion of a two-state resolution is in a state of suspended animation. U.S. Secretary of State Hillary Clinton has not been able to re-start talks. There is no prospective agreement on the status of East Jerusalem, the Temple Mount, the Arab refugees, and the future of Israeli settlements in the West Bank. The Palestinians demand that Israel should stop excavations around the Temple Mount. Israeli concessions have not brought Arab concessions.

In the near future, the Israeli government looks to the strengthening of a supportive Palestinian Authority and the preservation of a democratic government in Lebanon. Most Israelis continue to favor substantial withdrawals over time to avoid Israeli rule over a majority Palestinian population. At this time, most Israelis believe that any realignment plan to take Israel out of most of West Bank territories must avoid giving any ruling authority a veto over basic Israeli interests.

Hopefully, the Palestinian Authority and Hamas, based respectively in the West Bank and Gaza, might over time work out their differences to help bring about a two-state structure with the assurance of Israeli security.

I suggested that a NATO force be established on Israeli's borders to secure an peace. This might be preceded by the deployment of a peace-keeping force by the European Union. A new Palestinian state will also require $10 billion a year from Western nations for the foreseeable future.

Abbas' Position

In the wake of Hamas' seizure of Gaza, Abbas of the Palestinian Authority acted to dissolve the Hamas government in Gaza, which promptly rejected his action for a caretaker government for Gaza and the West Bank. In May, 2006, Abbas called for a referendum on a proposal that would recognize Israel on the basis of pre-1967 borders. Abbas also called for an international force to supervise a referendum in Gaza. At this point, armed conflict is continuing between the Palestinian Authority and Hamas in both the West Bank and Gaza. Hamas criticizes Fatah for negotiating with Israel and for failing to push for war crimes prosecutions against Israel following the invasion of Gaza in December, 2008.

The Fatah Party in the West Bank is barring residents of Gaza from annual pilgrimages to Mecca. The Palestinian Authority is now cutting off the salaries of Hamas officials in local governments in the West Bank. Fatah leaders had agreed to remove from the PLO charter the reference to the removal of Israel, and were prepared to divide the West Bank. It should be noted that Fatah has still not formally recognized Israel, and will not refer to Israel as a Jewish state. The August, 2009 Fatah convention reasserted a hard-line toward Israel. Abbas said there would be no negotiation with Israel while Jewish settlements continue to be built, and looks to the UN to recognize a Palestinian state without Israel's agreement. There is no constructive force for a two-state resolution in place of Fatah and Hamas. Abbas is so weak that he is threatening resignation, which would destroy the Palestinian Authority.

It remains to be seen whether ongoing peace might follow from a possible negotiated Israeli settlement with the Palestinian Authority as the interim government in the West Bank. I again underscore the need for an ongoing central role for the United States with a proposed NATO presence. Meanwhile, Israel maintains over-all security control in the West Bank.

Delayed Road-Map Negotiations

A two-state structure may need to be developed within the framework of a revised Road-map, with Israel on one side and the development of joint Fatah-Hamas rule over the next four years. Fatah and Hamas must bring about a cease-fire as a basis for the lifting of Israel's siege of Gaza. Hamas' need for funds to reconstruct Gaza has led to meetings with Fatah in Cairo and the prospect of a new election in Gaza and the West Bank. Israel's possible release of its prisoner Marwan Barghouti might advance reconciliation talks between Fatah and Hamas.

Former Israeli Prime Minister Olmert had met with Abbas and the heads of Egypt, Jordan and Saudi Arabia. Israel had released selected Fatah prisoners and removed other Fatah militiamen from its wanted list based on their surrender of weapons and written pledges of non-violence. Egypt would open crossings into Gaza if Fatah is present at these crossings. The Israeli security cabinet agreed to work with Egypt on an ongoing truce, but remained prepared to attack Gaza if the talks fail.

Most Israelis believe that a status quo is neither peaceful or secure, and want the United States and the Arab League to help broker negotiations based on the Road-map, and without the participation of Hamas. Israel's disengagement from most of the West Bank must be based on the assumption of governmental responsibility by the Palestinians on the basis of a negotiated settlement with a timetable within a 10-year armistice or hudna.

Economic Development in the West Bank

Currently, former British Prime Minister Tony Blair is coordinating efforts to strengthen Palestinian institutions to build a nation. He will not replace Washington as a mediator, and will work to develop an economic foundation for a Palestinian state. Down the line, an economic Marshall Plan ought to be developed, following the $7 billion pledged in 2007 by eighty nations for West Bank development. Netanyahu will cooperate with Blair in the building of industrial zones in the West Bank, with the aim of cutting back on border checkpoints to facilitate trade with Israel. Israel has opened a new vehicle crossing to Jenin to facilitate movement of Israeli Arabs into the West Bank. Israel is interested in opening trade offices in Arab countries.

The United States is planning a $500 million mortgage company to build ten new neighborhoods. The Obama Administration will give $300 million to nongovernmental organizations in Gaza for reconstruction, avoiding Hamas. In Jenin in the West Bank, Palestinian security officials have restored order as a model for cooperation between Palestinian and Israeli businessmen. At the same time, the Palestinian Prime Minister Salam Fayyad, under President Abbas, is working with Tony Blair on economic development.

Blair's success is reflected in the increase in Palestinian investment and trade, the reduction of Israeli checkpoints, and the growth of the new Palestinian National Security Force in the West Bank. Israel will not leave the West Bank before the Palestinian police take effective control. The opening of a second cell-phone by the Wataniya company is the largest foreign investment in the Palestinian economy.

Along with a NATO presence, the emergence of a Palestinian state depends on the development of a vibrant Palestinian society. An economic Marshall Plan for Palestinians will help transform this society, and develop a bottom-up impetus for lasting peace with Israel.

EFFORTS AT NEGOTIATED SETTLEMENT

The Arab League Seeks Negotiation

In March, 2007, member states of the Arab League agreed to the recognition of Israel and resumption of diplomatic relations if Israel would withdraw to pre-1967 borders, and give up the Golan and East Jerusalem. This follows Egyptian and Jordanian recognition of Israel. With limited support by President Obama, the Arab League has continued to seek Israel's withdrawal to pre-1967 borders, which is supported by Egypt. At the same time, Egypt supports the dissolution of Hamas as a threat to Sinai, and has limited the passage of weapons on its border with Gaza.

The Arab League also called for a solution to the problem of Palestinian refugees, without calling for full return to Israel. In October, 2008, Egypt and Saudi Arabia revived the Arab League proposal. But the Arab League said there would be no talks unless Israel stops all settlement construction.

At the same time, an Arab League resolution at the United Nations in December, 2008 condemned Israeli air attacks. The United States rejected this resolution as being one-sided, and called for an immediate cease-fire and halt to Hamas rocket threats. This is part of the American support of Fatah. At the same time, Hezbollah remained quiet during the Israel invasion of Gaza. Britain has resumed talks with Hezbollah, and its Prime Minister supports more troops going into Afghanistan. The visit of the Pope to Jordan, Israel and the West Bank in May, 2009 may further negotiations on a two-state resolution on the basis of Israel's right to exist. But the Arab League will not negotiate if settlement construction continues. President Obama has urged both sides to continue to negotiate on "final status" issues.

I support an official emissary from the United States to visit Arab capitals and Israel. President Obama has appointed George Mitchell who had established a power-sharing arrangement between Catholics and Protestants in North Ireland. Mitchell has met with Netanyahu, and advised that the United States strongly supports a two-state solution. Mitchell stressed that new Jewish settlements in the West Bank must be halted. Mitchell has referred to Israel as a Jewish state. But Mitchell has not made progress in his talks. Obama met with Netanyahu on May 18, and supports East Jerusalem as capital of the new Palestinian state.

I stressed that any Israeli withdrawal from most of the West Bank must be on the basis of assurances that the West Bank will not become the site of rocket attacks against central Israeli cities. Also, there must be recognition by Fatah of all prior peace agreements, the strengthening of legal Jewish settlement blocs in the West Bank, and shared administration in East Jerusalem, which would remain under Israel control. Netanyahu supports continued Jewish construction in East Jerusalem, including the Gilo and Nof Zion sections. There has been no progress on the status of East Jerusalem or the Palestinian refugees.

Except for the status of East Jerusalem, these terms are generally acceptable to the European Union, the United States, and the United Nations. This calls for a true Palestinian ideological transformation. The European Union strongly supports the resumption of "land-for-peace" talks.

CONCLUSION

In conclusion, Israel must depend on itself to counter terrorism by mobilizing its citizens, and decide where and when to retaliate against attacks. This can change only when NATO establishes itself on the West Bank and Gaza borders as a monitoring force in defense of democratic values in the Middle East. After years of conflict, Egypt and Jordan have recognized Israel, and Israel looks to Syria to follow this precedent.

I wish to quote Abraham Foxman, National Director of the Anti-Defamation League, on Jewish settlements in the West Bank. "Saying that Israel will never give up the settlements ignores the fact that former Prime Minister Ehud Barak offered to dismantle 80 percent of the settlements at Camp David; that his successor, Ariel Sharon, dismantled all of the settlements in Gaza; and that Israeli leaders have repeatedly indicated that most of the settlements will go if there is peace. . . ."

In December/January 2008–2009, Israel launched an invasion of Gaza, fighting against Hamas whose ranks are made up grandchildren of Arabs who attacked the newly-created state of Israel in 1948. The invasion followed numerous Israeli raids into Gaza after 2005. After inflicting severe damage in villages and towns in Gaza, Israel declared a unilateral cease-fire, and withdrew its troops from Gaza. It should be noted that a dozen Arab states boycotted an emergency summit meeting of the Arab League during Israel's invasion. By criticizing Israel for its invasion of Gaza, Arabs are denying its right to exist.

Israel is being sharply criticized for the killing of civilians in Gaza. Yet Hamas used civilians as shields, and abused Red Cross symbols. Israel's military maintains that the invasion of Gaza did not violate international law since it was directed against terrorists. Meanwhile, the Palestinian Authority, which is not now interested in talks with Israel until all new construction is halted, is seeking to turn world opinion against the Jewish state.

Israel and the United States signed an agreement to seek to stop the rearming of Hamas through Egypt. The United States and Israel should now look to the permanent reopening of the Egypt's border crossings in cooperation with Fatah and European monitors. United States equipment and technical assistance are needed to monitor the entire Israel-Gaza border. If rocket attacks continue, Israel should be prepared to reoccupy the entire border between Gaza and Israel on a long-term basis to stop the digging of tunnels.

George J. Mitchell was appointed by President Obama to maintain a Gaza truce, and has met with Olmert, Netanyahu, and Abbas of the Palestinian Authority to discuss a two-state resolution. He has not met with Hamas and Syrian leaders, and will meet with Egyptian and Jordanian leaders. The failure of the Arab League to deal with Iran gives President Obama the opportunity to take the initiative in Middle East affairs. Obama favors limiting further Jewish settlement in the West Bank, seeks the end of the Gaza blockade, and the removal of checkpoints on the basis of assurances of Israel's security. Israel seeks the containment of Iran and Hamas as a basis for a settlement freeze.

Israel's invasion of Gaza demonstrated the capability of its soldiers, and the spirit of the homefront. The government demonstrated its capacity for responsibility and planning. These elements must continue to be exercised in the ongoing effort for a two-state resolution of the present situation in cooperation with the Palestinian Authority. This calls for the suppression of Hamas as a terrorist organization, with the cooperation of NATO nations. The containment of Iran must proceed to enable negotiations to continue for a two-state resolution.

Egypt and Jordan should have a leading role in the emergence of a Palestinian state. If Egyptian-backed peace talks should fail at this time, Israel is expected to re-invade Gaza to stop rocket attacks. Meanwhile, Hamas continues to demand the lifting of the Israeli economic embargo in Gaza, and seeks the release of Hamas prisoners in Israel in exchange for captive Corporal Gilad Shalit.

Israel looks to the Palestinian Authority to develop a professional military force capable of taking control of Gaza with the cooperation of Israel and the United States. This would lead to recognition of Israel by the governing authority in Gaza. Now NATO is conducting a major military operation in Afghanistan to oust the Taliban militants. This will offset the withdrawal of American forces from Iraq. The United States should continue to use non-pilot drone aircraft to attack militants in Pakistan and Afghanistan.

Chapter Eight

Scriptwriting

My ongoing effort at the writing and marketing of numerous scripts began on a high note in 1957, when the prestigious William Morris Agency signed me to a contract for a live television play, "Ticket to Tripani." The script deals with the winning by a milk delivery man, in a city-wide Catholic church lottery, of passage to his Sicilian hometown. He promptly encounters the resistance of his family to the voyage, marked by the upcoming marriage of his daughter. The winner's wife details all the other disruptions that his departure would bring, until he is almost convinced to reject the prize. At the end, his humdrum life and daily work routine become quite unbearable in contrast to the illusion of a once-in-a-lifetime opportunity to return to the land of his birth and early dreams. He finally demands his ticket to Tripani.

The marketing efforts of the William Morris Agency were not successful. This led to my preparation of new scripts, and representation by the Jack Scagnetti Literary Agency. Over time, my materials became more dated and required revisions for any successful presentation and marketing. As television drama and motion pictures became more and more violent, my scripts remained involved with the presentation of family and individual values and portrayals. An exception was an action drama, "Sandcastle," which was initially requested by New Line Cinema, Columbia Tri-Star Pictures, Universal City Studios and the Zanuck Company. I also developed a children's book series based on a TV script, "Joppolo," the story of a wooden toy clown in a department store surrounded by futuristic robots and high fashion dolls.

Through my presidency of Dropsie University, I met Lionel Pincus of G.M. Warburg Pincus & Co., who subsequently put me in contact with Dr. Harold Brown, on the board of directors of the Mattel Company, manufacturers of the Barbie doll. I suggested the incorporation of Barbie in my TV and book materials. However, Bob Hudnut, a Vice President of the Mattel Company, advised the firm would become involved only on the basis of the sale of the concept to a publisher/producer.

My efforts with children's book publishers included Harper Children's Group, Bantam Doubleday Dell, Dutton's Children's Books and Random House. Producers of children's TV materials included Children's BBC, the Nickelodeon Channel and Fox Family Television.

In 2004, I was called by Ricky Corradi, Vice President-International Department of Mondo TV in Rome. He advised his firm would be prepared to handle production of the "Joppolo" TV show in its home studio on the basis of joint funding by a second producer in exchange for 50% of worldwide rights.

I also attempted to market my "Joppolo" book series among software game producers, including Sega of America, Sony Computer Entertainment, Zeek Interactive, Infogrames, 4Kids and the Hasbro Toy Group.

SANDCASTLE

On a more hopeful note, on April 23, 2009, I was advised by the Executive Vice President for Corporate Communications at Time Warner, Inc. that my action script "Sandcastle" was forwarded to the appropriate department for consideration.

I had submitted the script for "Sandcastle" on March 8, 2009, with the following lengthy summary:

Mortimer Cain, a Hollywood mogul, has exclusive rights for the recovery of a Spanish treasure chest on a California island. He brought huge equipment and his studio assistants to the island on the basis of a purported sixteenth century map pinpointing the location of the doubloons. After as yet unsuccessful drillings, Cain criticizes the archaeologist who defends the authenticity of the pigskin scroll. Through his binoculars, Cain observes Veronica, a starlet, who strikes a treasure chest while building a sandcastle on the beach. Cain orders his secretary to take full notes of all ensuing events for the development of a movie script, which would recoup all his drilling costs and gossip column ridicule.

Victoria transfers the doubloons to her picnic box, and asks Zacharia, a beachcomber lying nearby, to help carry the treasure to her power boat. Cain observes that the boat is marked "Coronado Marina," where he will pursue Victoria. The starlet and her escort, carrying the picnic box, check into the said del Coronado Hotel in San Diego. They place the treasure in the safe deposit box in her room. Meanwhile, Cain and his entourage register at the hotel desk. On his cell phone, Cain calls his driver and other studio vehicles. To avoid detection, Victoria and Zacharia dress incognito, and slip into a meeting of Japan businessmen.

Cain orders a studio aide, Bubbles, to scout the hotel to find Zacharia. The hotel manager protests the lack of decorum of Cain's entourage. To avoid scrutiny, Victoria and Zacharia slip into a wedding rehearsal, and get caught up in a dispute between the families of the bride and groom. Slipping out of the hotel, Victoria and Zacharia cut through a file of marching U.S. Marines, and grab fatigue uniforms and helmets from a Marine truck. They fall in line with the trainees, and away from Cain's scrutiny.

Back in the hotel, where they spend the night, Victoria and Zacharia move the doubloons from the safe deposit box into Victoria's station wagon. But they are detected by one of Cain's aides, who follows the station wagon by taxi, and calls Cain. Promptly, Cain orders his assistants into their cars for the pursuit. He also orders helicopters to film the chase from above.

Victoria and Zacharia bury the doubloons in a crevasse and push the station wagon off a cliff. They enter a nearby inn, and come upon an orgiastic scene of a king's court with a throne and walls lined by armor and torture racks. There is a court jester and dancing girls. Victoria confesses to Zacharia that she had been in close contact with Cain's secretary to stage the coastal chase, leading to the inn. Bubbles promptly appears to try to entice Zacharia over Victoria's objection.

Victoria, Zacharia, Cain, and his secretary finally meet in San Francisco. The secretary admits that when she asked Victoria to build the sandcastle, she was not aware that Cain had buried the doubloons at the site on the beach. Indeed, the doubloons were all trinkets supplied by the prop department. And Zacharia advises that he is actually a reporter from the local newspaper, assigned to report on Cain's digging. Cain indicates he will now resume the search for the real doubloons.

Back on the island where the sandcastle was built, several Marine landing craft hit the beach. Digging slit trenches, the Marines come upon the real buried treasure. Cain waves the map, shouting that he has exclusive rights to any findings on the island—the U.S. Marines notwithstanding

Later, at the del Coronado Hotel, Victoria and Zacharia are having drinks with the bride and groom who had been rehearsing their wedding. The bride admits she is going to have a baby, and Victoria indicates she had lost her innocence at the hotel. It is now wedding time for Victoria and Zacharia in a world that is a stage, orchestrated by Mortimer Cain.

I had also advised Time Warner that Activision, the interactive software game producer, requested to be advised about definitive entertainment commitments for the project.

MEASURE OF GUILT

The following is a description of my drama by a reader for Storm Entertainment in Santa Monica, CA:

AUTHOR: Joseph Rappaport
TITLE: *Measure of Guilt*
GENRE: Drama
LOCATION: High Falls in Upper Nebraska

LOGLINE: An ex-football star who is down on his luck gets into a scuffle at a local tavern in the small town of High Falls, Nebraska, but the scuffle turns into accidental murder and now police and vigilantes are on his trail as he runs for his life.

SYNOPSIS: *Measure of Guilt* opens in a tavern in the small town of High Falls, Nebraska. TOMMY CASPER, an ex-football quarterback, is drinking and talking to some of the locals. Since disappointing the town by breaking his knee in his first game for the university, Tommy has been working driving an old bulldozer. The locals are criticizing Tommy for undercutting JIM MCINTYRE, his competition. McIntyre has a new bulldozer and has been spreading the word that Tommy's work is substandard. Tommy has had enough and tells the locals to go ahead and tell McIntyre to "bug off," then exits the tavern.

That evening, Tommy goes to the bus station to meet his friend, MALONE. While he waits, he runs into MR. and MRS. DONALDSON. They are waiting for their daughter, SUSAN DONALDSON, to arrive on the bus from out of town. The conversation is awkward because Tommy used to date Susan. Mr. Donaldson refuses to even look at Tommy. Malone arrives and Tommy greets him. As they leave, Tommy runs into Susan. He says hello, but quickly exits with Malone.

Back at the tavern, Tommy and Malone have a drink and catch up on old times. They talk about Mr. Donaldson and how supportive he was of Tommy prior to his broken knee. Malone is the football player who tackled Tommy and hurt him. They had since become friends, and Malone had even lent Tommy money to buy his bulldozer because he had felt so bad. Meanwhile, Jim McIntyre is in the tavern as well. He is being given the message from Tommy to "bug off." This angers McIntyre and he approaches Tommy. Tommy does not want to fight, but after McIntyre pushes him around a bit, Malone can't stand it and jumps in and begins fighting Jim. Tommy tries to break it up as Malone pounds McIntyre. McIntyre falls and hits his head on a table. The blow kills him.

Malone and Tommy are now on the run. They are traveling through the woods until they come upon ELLEN SIMPSON's house. Ellen spends a lot of time at the tavern and is a friend of Tommy's. She has no choice but to let them in when Malone produces a pistol from his pocket. Malone yanks Ellen's telephone line from the wall. Tommy believes they should turn themselves in to JEREMY FOSTER, the justice of the peace. Jeremy is also a friend of Tommy's, and Tommy believes that Malone would be treated fairly due to the fact that it was an accident. Malone is not interested in this idea. He wants to flee, and Tommy feels obliged to stick by his side.

Jeremy Foster visits the Donaldsons' home when he learns of what has happened. Mr. Donaldson thinks that they should let the police deal with Tommy. Jeremy is trying to convince him that Tommy will be killed before he can go to trial because vigilantes are looking for him as well. Jeremy wants to give Tommy a chance and hopes that others will support him. Then Jeremy talks to Mr. Donaldson alone. He tells him he knows that Mr. Donaldson and Ellen Simpson had an affair, and that Tommy knew about it. Jeremy asks Mr. Donaldson not to hold a grudge and to join him in sticking close to the state troopers so that they can be the voices of reason on Tommy's behalf. Mr. Donaldson is still not convinced.

Back at Ellen Simpson's, Malone is becoming agitated. He is a cocaine user, and he is nervous and quick to pull his gun out and point it at Ellen, and even Tommy. He is angry with Tommy for not sticking up for himself. Tommy is angry with Malone for getting involved instead of just exiting the tavern with him. Suddenly, outside, a telephone repairman shows up, most likely because the phone company detected the damaged line when Malone ripped it out of the wall. Malone fires his gun through the front door at the man. The man gets away in his truck.

Now the police know where Tommy and Malone are holed up. The police surround Ellen Simpson's house and prepare for a showdown. The CHIEF knows that they may have a hostage situation and is working out the details on how to approach the house. Jeremy Foster is Tommy Casper's character witness and is there trying to convince the Chief to take Tommy alive. However, WILLY GREGG, the man who provoked McIntyre to approach Tommy, is painting Tommy as a criminal. Jeremy requests that the Chief let him in the house to talk Tommy into coming out, but the Chief will not allow it.

By this time, Malone is raving mad due in large part to the effect of drugs. He is talking about running through the police blockage and over the mountain to "touch the sky." He wants to use Ellen as a hostage. Malone begins to lose it. There is a struggle between Tommy and Malone, and Tommy gains control of the gun, while Malone breaks down in tears. Tommy decides to wait for Malone to calm down before they turn themselves in.

Outside, Mr. Donaldson has shown up. Mr. Donaldson is there to support Jeremy for the sake of Susan. As Jeremy, Mr. Donaldson and other locals discuss the situation and share their thoughts about Tommy, Susan shows up.

Inside, Tommy is promising Malone that he will support him, when a familiar voice calls out. Tommy looks out the window to see Susan running towards the house. She is warning that police are coming in the house through the basement. Tommy opens the front door. Malone grabs a candleholder and runs for the door as well.

Tommy steps outside to tell Susan to get away. Just then, Malone steps out, threatening to kill Susan. He is instantly shot dead. Tommy retreats back inside the house.

Inside, Tommy tells Ellen to leave, but she will not. She wants to help him. Then Jeremy Foster enters the house to try to talk Tommy into coming out. Now

Ellen leaves. Outside the police become nervous when it takes a long time, so they shoot tear gas into the house. After carrying Jeremy outside, Tommy is arrested.

At the trial, Tommy is given six months in jail for being an accomplice and running from the law. Susan visits Tommy in jail where they talk about the aftermath. Jeremy is in the hospital, damaged due to smoke inhalation. Mr. Donaldson has split with Mrs. Donaldson. Susan wants to leave town with Tommy when he gets out, but he says that he would like to stay here in High Falls. He wants to face up to his critics and eventually gain the respect he had when he was the captain quarterback of the football team.

COMMENTS: As it is often said in the study of literature, strong characters make for a strong story. The character, in fact, *is* the story. *Measure of Guilt* is strong in that it goes to great pains to tell the story of Tommy Casper and his personal pain.

We care about Tommy's plight. We are introduced to his world in the beginning as we find him drinking in a bar, defending his shabby work to a bunch of lowlifes. Then we learn from where he has fallen. He was on a pedestal. He was a star. And in an instant, he became a nobody in the eyes of his former supporters. He is even blamed for the accident that took him out of football forever.

Malone is also interesting. His past mistakes and his guilt over injuring Tommy has sent his life down dark paths, and now he feels compelled to befriend Tommy. They are two of a kind. When Malone kills Jim McIntyre, it is guilt and circumstance that keeps them together to the very end.

Despite the strong characters and interesting premise however, there are problems that prevent this story from being workable as a feature film. Had the story been written in proper screenplay format, the story would most likely have ended up on nearly half the amount of pages. Each page in a story written in proper format represents roughly a minute of screen time. It's simply too short to be a feature.

Looking beyond the simple observations, we need to examine the style in which the screenplay is written. Heavy use of dialogue with very little description. The description that is there tends to be done through dialogue. Also, there is a repetition of sentiments. In real life, we might tell the same story to four or five people, but movie audiences don't want to watch this repetition. The dialogue is very realistic, but too time-consuming. The pace needs to be picked up, and the dialogue cleaned up so that we are left only with lines of dialogue that move the story along.

Another comment on the dialogue, and then an offer of a solution: There is a great story told through the dialogue. Tommy's climb to the top. Tommy's downfall after the accident. Tommy's Regional Plan with Susan. Tommy's relationship with Malone before and after the accident. Mr. Donaldson's affair with Ellen Simpson. This is a wonderful combination of sub-stories that contributes to the whole and would be interesting to watch. We are robbed of that when each story is told only through dialogue. We want to see this. It's good stuff.

Within the dialogue of *Measure of Guilt* are the makings of a wonderful drama. A rewrite that brings the real story closer to the forefront will greatly do it justice.

RECOMMENDATION: NEEDS A REWRITE IN PROPER SCREENPLAY FORMAT WITH A FOCUS UPON THE STORY THAT IS CURRENTLY TOLD PRIMARILY THROUGH DIALOGUE.

JOPPOLO

The following is a description of my TV special:

Joppolo the clown is presented as a floor model in a toy department, surrounded by futuristic robots and high fashion dolls. We listen to the conversations between the clown and an old floor sweeper who tries to attract people to Joppolo. A young salesman is torn between the clown and the robots. After the department manager makes arrangements to return the clown to the warehouse, the sweeper steals Joppolo, and brings the clown to the apartment he shares with his son's family. When the arrested sweeper is brought to the police station, the cops begin singing songs to the clown. A newspaper account leads to a public demand for small replicas of Joppolo, who is returned to the toy department as a permanent floor model. Now customers are talking to the clown, as in the old days, in the same way as little girls have always been speaking to their dolls. The old sweeper observes the scene happily. I have written a 15-chapter book for young people on Joppolo's adventures in the toy department.

I received the following comments by a script analyst:
I like the idea of an older toy competing with newer toys, and the value of children using their imagination when playing with toys. Good stuff.

Yet I'm still not completely sure how Joppolo and Andrew communicate. Do they talk to one another? Can Joppolo only communicate with kids who believe in him? If so, this must be clear.

It's good that you have Andrew called in to meet with Cheeves early in the script—this conflict should be set up early. But can Cheeves give Andrew an ultimatum? Perhaps Andrew must sell at least ten robots by the end of the week or Cheeves will put Andrew in a different department . . . which may mean it's to the woodpile for Joppolo.

Whichever ultimatum you choose, it must be established early, and be the goal of the script. Since the script is so short, the goal should be set up right away and Andrew should go about trying to achieve that goal—but fail throughout.

What is Andrew's goal? Andrew seems to lament the robots, and long for kids to accept a toy like Joppolo, but when a kid finally does, Andrew won't let him go. Why is that? If we are to sympathize with Andrew, then we must really care about his plight. Can you show that Andrew didn't have any toys growing up, and just had to play with a brick? Or something to that effect.

In the end then, more Joppolos are made to avoid a PR incident? But how does that drive up the demand? If Andrew "wins" just because bad publicity was created for the store, it doesn't seem as rewarding for the character as it should be. Put Andrew through some trials—have bad things happen to him, even more—and when he emerges on top in the end, make it from his own work, not by happenstance.

A POOR KIND OF CREATURE

The following is a summary of the script:

In a colonial mansion outside Brattleboro, Harry Kimball, the dissipate scion of the family fortune, criticizes his sister's infatuation with show business. Flora declares that the theatre, installed in the barn across the yard, will bring music and laughter to the staid old Kimball estate and into their lives. Harry cannot forgive himself for giving his sister ownership of the barn.

Enter Koko Freeman, the rotund comic with his red hat; his manager Jack Feivel; and Fish, the short, thin actor, with large glasses. Defensively, Koko goes into his characteristic spin as he comments on all the reasons why he chose to bring his comic play to Vermont, including his manager's failure to get him a featured booking in Vegas.

Shocked by his repartee, Flora says she had a far different impression of Koko in his portrayal of Shylock from Shakespeare's "Merchant of Venice" on TV Startime. On television, his wig and cape and camera shots contrasted with his real-life appearance. Jack Feivel deplores Koko's theatrical aspirations, and Flora doubts that he will be able to move across the yard to a real stage.

Koko: "What do you want the theatre for? Listen. The theatre is a woman. For Koko. With satin and cloth. Sparkles. And a painted face." Flora replies she will not permit Koko to bring his comic style to her stage.

Enter Marcia Hendrickson, the aging blond songstress of the Johnny Carson show, who is now attempting a comeback on the stage. Her appearance restores life and vigor to Harry Kimball, who welcomes her to the Kimball estate.

Koko imitates Marcia's ineptitude, and shakes his head in disbelief that he himself is embarking on an effort at the theatre. When the others leave, Koko faces Flora alone. She admits that she and Koko share the same illusion about the stage—and the same uncertainty about each other.

Koko later says to Feivel: "I'm going from monologue to dialogue. Is this clear to you? So I can spit out one line. That will stab me in the head. And come from my own heart." Koko is prepared to let Fish take up his comic style.

Meanwhile, Harry Kimball and Marcia Hendrickson plot to replace Koko on the stage with evenings of song.

Flora tentatively offers Koko her theatre—without Marcia Hendrickson—only if he would bring in a writer to rework the play throughout the summer in the manner of his appearance on TV Startime. Yet, Koko wonders whether he himself could really change—with his fat face, peephole eyes, and wild hair. Flora replies that with integrity on the sage, she would accept Koko no matter how he looks.

Flora comments on the emptiness of her own life and of Koko's. Flora: "Somehow you've made it up to now. Without attempting to act. And Flora Kimball has failed to achieve her own being . . . I think we're so pathetic. You and I . . . For what we can aspire, there's be a theatre. For you. And for me."

Koko and Feivel argue over their future. Koko: "What is it with you, Feivel? You come to Vermont—you get an attack of hayfever. I get praise for TV Startime—you tell me I shouldn't go on without my red hat. I'm not a monkey, with an organ grinder—collecting money in the street . . . An imitator is a poor kind of creature. He throws out jokes, and the yaks from the table hit him in the face."

Alone on the stage, Koko utters lines from his appearance on TV Startime. In contrast, he also goes into an introduction to one of his night club appearances.

Later in the theatre with Koko, Flora portrays the contrasts in her life between the Kimball mansion and the Kimball Playhouse. Flora: "Will the real Flora Kimball stand up?" Flora recalls how she came down from the room above the theatre and stood on the stage. She recited from The Merry Wives of Windsor: "Sir, let me speak with you in your chamber—you shall hear how things go; and, I warrant, to your content."

Knowing that Flora will not permit her stage to be used for cheap comedy, Harry Kimball advises Marcia he will manage her comeback as a singer—starting in the Kimball Playhouse.

In the theatre, Harry attacks Koko's mockery. Harry: "Miss Hendrickson was America's songstress. While you were telling your filthy, little jokes. You comic. You sloven fool." Koko orders Harry off the stage. Koko: "This is not a bordello. This is a theatre!" Flora won't give her stage to Marcia either.

Later, when Koko and Flora walk into the theatre, she repeats that Koko can stay in the room above for the whole summer. Other scheduled troupes and ensembles will appear on the stage, while Koko and a writer would recast the play and himself. Just as he did when he portrayed Shylock. Flora offers to show the room to Koko. The comedian follows her, shouting: "Wait for me!"

The script was requested, with interest in coproduction, by Universal City Studios and Fine Line Features. Letters expressing interest in distribution were received from New Line Cinema, Orion Pictures, Showcase Entertainment and the Overseas Filmgroup.

After 1999, I was increasingly engaged in commercial real estate sales as a source of additional income, which continues to this day.

Appendix

Project Proposal

1984
MARCH OF DIMES BIRTH DEFECTS FOUNDATION
AMERICAN ASSOCIATION OF COLLEGES OF NURSING
AMERICAN COLLEGE OF OBSTETRICIANS
AND GYNECOLOGISTS

DEVELOPMENT OF CORE COMPETENCIES IN
MATERNAL/INFANT CONTENT IN
UNDERGRADUATE NURSING EDUCATION

SUMMARY

The March of Dimes and the two co-sponsoring (non-budgeted) organizations propose a project for the development and evaluation of a core competencies framework for the maternal/infant component in baccalaureate nursing education to prepare students to provide more effective early and continuous prenatal care to pregnant women including those from special cultural and socioeconomic backgrounds. Maternal/infant morbidity and mortality need to be addressed by the increased use of technology, the further regionalization of levels of perinatal service, and an aggressive approach to risk assessment and preventive care particularly during the first trimester. However, the severe shortage of skilled perinatal nurses limits the potential of these measures to improve pregnancy outcomes and the health of newborns. Current perinatal content in schools of nursing may be a root cause of the inability of the states to provide sufficient professional personnel for the technological and organizational resources that are at hand. Undergraduate instruction must address this dichotomy by examining curriculum and teaching methodologies in maternal/child health. This effort has the potential of increasing the number of entry-level practitioners in maternal/infant nursing, as well as the number of students in perinatal graduate programs. The goal of the project will be the preparation and demonstration of core competencies that will: 1) Develop an understanding of the needs of special population groups that pose high-risk problems in the public health field, to increase the skill of the beginning level practitioner in relation to diverse individual, adolescent, working women and lifestyle situations; 2) Provide a theoretical and clinical basis for effective beginning-level perinatal practice to help the states to meet the service and technological demands particularly of high-risk maternal/fetal, maternal/newborn, and neonatal situations; 3) Develop a sound comprehension in the student nurse of the elements of assessment, planning, implementation and evaluation in primary perinatal care programs extended through public health facilities. Another vital benefit will be the development of new curricular materials, guidebooks and manuals as teaching aids in the education of nurses. In the first year, the project will survey and analyze current curriculums and teaching mythologies used in 300 baccalaureate schools of nursing to prepare students for maternal-infant nursing; develop a definition of competencies necessary for effective clinical and community-based practice; and identify those schools which have implemented a range of competencies. A panel of specialists will be convened to define the full range of competencies, and make recommendations on the development of a survey tool which will determine what is currently being taught and how. The next 12 months will refine the competencies and develop a self-assessment tool for schools. These will proceed from requests for further information from schools that have incorporated a range of competencies, site visits to these schools, and another meeting of the panel. The last phase (12 months) will include the preparation of guidelines for the implementation of the model; the convening of four regional meetings for dissemination of information; and the identification of sites for implementation of a pilot program. The implementation guidelines will describe how the teaching of perinatal nursing can be incorporated in the full length of a general course of instruction, and how didactic and clinical elements should be integrated to best prepare students for early and ongoing prenatal care including services for women who customarily have delayed or avoided such care. The core competencies framework, implementation plan, and demonstration model will be evaluated by independent specialists who will be asked to review the end products from the standpoint of content, design, applicability, and learning outcome. The project will provide to schools of nursing data and analysis on what is presently being taught on maternal/infant care, core competencies, a tool for self-assessment, teaching plan, and (following the 3-year grant period) the results and evaluation of pilot demonstrations.

CONTENTS

Project Narrative

Table Referencing Criteria for Evaluating Applications

V.   Adaptation and Use of the Results
     V-A
     V-B
VI. Capabilities of Applicant
     VI-A
     VI-B

PROJECT NARRATIVE

Introduction

The three co-sponsor organizations propose a 3 year project for the development and evaluation of a core competencies framework for the maternal/infant component in baccalaureate nursing education.

On the basis of a survey of more than 300 schools of nursing offering four-year professional studies, the co-sponsors will define the competencies necessary for beginning practitioners for the delivery of effective early and continuous perinatal care; develop a tool for nursing school self-assessment; disseminate information through a series of regional conferences; and identify sites for pilot programs utilizing the competencies.

Once the competencies are delineated, continuing education will be the mechanism by which these behaviors can be integrated in present practice. As present practitioners become competent, continuing education can further define programs that will increase expertise in the area of maternal/infant health.

Graduate programs will be able to use the competency statements to diagnose student learning needs until such time that the competencies are integrated in undergraduate education. Graduate education can subsequently design curriculums to build upon these competencies to insure better-prepared practitioners and educators.

The project addresses a range of regional and national priorities set forth by the Division of Maternal and Child Health. It is designed to help meet the nationwide shortage of clinical and public health nurses able to provide effective early and continuous prenatal care, work with new medical technologies, and fulfill the health personnel needs of regionalized perinatal programs. The project focuses on improving the outcome of pregnancy and the health of the infant, with particular emphasis on special cultural and socioeconomic groups.

Core competencies to be developed will relate particularly to the assessment of risk factors for disease and disability during and after pregnancy and in the neonatal period, and prepare student nurses for the early identification, tracking and application of preventive measures. These measures are inherently cost effective as compared to the costs of care for disabled and diseased infants.

The preparation of competencies for the education of perinatal nurses also meets the DMCH priority emphasis on Special Studies for the development of guidance materials and protocols for risk identification during prenatal and infant periods, including studies of the application of behavioral psychology in the provision of maternal and child health care.

I. PROBLEM IDENTIFICATION, DESCRIPTION, DOCUMENTATION AND ANALYSIS

The United States is 18th in the international ranking of infant mortality. Major causes of infant deaths and complications include prematurity and low birth weight, infection, respiratory complications, and birth injuries. Maternal morbidity and mortality result primarily from hypertensive disorders of pregnancy,hemorrhage, infection, heart disease, diabetes, and amniotic fluid embolism. Fetal death rates are higher among pregnant teenagers, women over 35 years of age, members of particular cultural minorities, and women in the lower socioeconomic group.

The December, 1980 Surgeon General's Workshop on Maternal and Infant Health[1] addressed this situation in a broad range of recommendations, with direct implications for the quality of the education of nurses, including the following:

- "There should be a national initiative to assure prenatal evaluation and counseling in the first trimester of pregnancy for all pregnant women."
- "All maternal and child health programs should have a strong mental health component which includes capacities for:
  a) Identification and recognition of the special cultural and other individual differences in family functioning and prenatal and early child care patterns to guarantee appropriate service availability and effectiveness.
  b) Provide expert consultation, including where appropriate, diagnosis and preventive planning to meet the needs of families where for a variety of reasons traditional clinical services are not available or are ineffective."
- "Policies of both public and private health care sectors should ensure that nutritional services become an integral part of health services for mothers and children."

- "The Surgeon General should bring together the relevant parties, such as, public health, nursing, medicine, nutrition and other health professionals to plan for the training of maternal and child health professionals. Service models for maternal and child health should be created as a basis for training and delivery of services."
- "Adolescents represent a special population with problems of sexuality, pregnancy and parenting. There should be special programs to meet the needs of this population to include health, education, social, nutritional and other support services."
- "Each State should develop a plan to make prenatal and parenting education available to all families during pregnancy and to those families with preschool infants."

In the three years following the Workshop recommendations, there has also been increased emphasis on the special health needs of pregnant women in the workplace, including the important role of public health nurses in dealing with these needs. The March of Dimes has been particularly active in this area through its "Good Health is Good Business" public education program, as well as its professional education grant to the American Association of Occupational Health Nurses to develop workshops in selected aspects of reproduction for Occupational Health Nurses.

The proposed grant will undertake the development of a core competencies framework and the dissemination of information and an implementation plan to meet evident needs for improved instruction in maternal and infant care as part of general nursing education. The proposed grant will meet the need to prepare student nurses to:

- assess high risk conditions in maternal and infant health care, particularly where many specialized services are not now rendered;
- relate to problems posed by special cultural and socioeconomic situations and lifestyles which are reflected in inadequate care in the first trimester of pregnancy and after;
- deal with the nutritional requirements of pregnant women and infants;
- provide early and continuous care for pregnant adolescents;
- provide for the health care needs of pregnant working women including those who are pregnant for the first time after the age of 30;
- adapt to the variety of community medicine and public health demands in the perinatal field.

Maternal/infant morbidity are being addressed by the increased use of high technology, the regionalization for perinatal services, and an aggressive approach to risk assessment and preventive care. However, the severe shortage of skilled perinatal nurses presently limits the potential of these measures for the early identification of risks and continuous care to improve pregnancy outcomes and the health of newborns.

There is a perception in the professional community that the inability of schools of nursing to provide sufficient professional personnel for available technological and organizational resources in Maternal/Infant Health Care is related to the quality and quantity of didactic study and clinical experience provided in undergraduate education. In addressing this dichotomy, schools of nursing would make a vital contribution to the achievement of cost-effective gains in prenatal care services.

Integration of core competencies into existing conceptional frameworks will help to assure a better prepared entry level practitioner to provide care to mothers and babies by providing a broader base of knowledge in public and community health as well as the acute care settings. Improved undergraduate instruction will also prepare and perhaps motivate nursing students for entry into graduate-level programs to specialize in Maternal/Infant Health. This in turn would produce better-qualified candidates for faculty positions in schools of nursing, and advanced practitioners for all health care settings.

Responses from 202 baccalaureate schools of nursing to a 1979 questionnaire by the University of North Carolina at Chapel Hill School of Nursing underscore the inadequacy of teaching strategies for maternal and infant health care in all the states, which our grant will address.

The respondents noted that most obstetrical theory was presented in the junior year, with very little of this content offered in the senior year. OB theory was generally presented in block fashion rather than integrated with related nursing study, and obstetrical nursing textbooks were generally regarded as inadequate.

There was wide disparity in OB clinical experiences, which were organized in non-integrated block form in inpatient and outpatient services. The respondents noted the lack of pattern and continuity in short-term intensive experiences with both mother and infant, nor were there sustained long-term contacts with the pregnant family. The directors of the survey concluded: "The current increased interest in the health care of women was not reflected in the nursing curricula we surveyed."[2]

A needs survey conducted by the Stony Brook (NY) School of Nursing in the Fall of 1981 found that over half of the 245 nurse educator-respondents had little confidence in their ability to teach high-risk maternal/newborn care.

A survey of nursing education in Canada in 1978–79 found that the care provided by new graduates for patients with complications in antepartum, intrapartum, and post-partum/newborn care settings frequently did not meet minimum standards. The inability of faculty to provide adequate instruction in the perinatal area was an underlying factor in this situation.

Intensive and expensive orientation of beginning practitioners has become a responsibility particularly of staff development units. The long period of time in transition from student to practitioner is due both to the ever-increasing amount of knowledge and complexity of medical and technical advances, and the strain that increasing knowledge has placed on content selection for the baccalaureate curriculum.

The recent initiation of the integrated curriculum provides the student with a framework within which theory for nursing practice is enveloped and in which the process of nursing bases its existence. The framework provides the faculty a common and specific meaning for the incorporation of content at every level of the curriculum, but has limited the amount of time previously spent in specific courses such as in maternal and child health. The framework permeates every aspect of the curriculum design and every learning experience (Torres and Yura; 1974). Recent graduates appear to have had fewer learning experiences in maternal-child health and nursing care of children than those of 5 years ago.[3]

We have received numerous testimonies from directors and teachers in the nursing field on the benefits that can be anticipated from our planned survey, (See Appendix A) definition of criteria, and development of a core competencies model.

"Talking with faculty across the country, I have found that they describe a large reduction of focus on all specialties in undergraduate curricula. This is logical since the stated goal is the nurse generalist. However, this does pose challenges for those of us concerned about high quality specialty practice. I will be happy to assist you in any way."

Professor of Nursing
Child Development and Mental
Retardation Center
University of Washington

"This project will make an important contribution to the care of mothers and infants by assuring that nurses who deliver this care are adequately prepared in their nursing programs. The development of integrated curriculums in nursing education has tended to reduce the amount of time devoted to maternal/infant care in many programs. Your proposal will focus attention on this important clinical area and assist educators to improve their curriculum offerings."

Dean, School of Nursing
College of New Rochelle

". . . we find that nurses coming out of school are not prepared for entry level positions. The degree of preparation and experience seems to be dependent upon the particular interest and area of expertise of the instructors in any given program."

School Health Consultant
Bureau of Maternal and Child Health
Arizona Department of Health Services

"The field of perinatal nursing is exploding with knowledge and becoming a significant area of nursing practice requiring multidimensional skills. The importance of this practice area in the nursing curriculum needs to be studied and evaluated as new graduates often report a cursory experience in the care of mothers, infants and children. In addition, the increasing amount of knowledge being developed on a daily basis requires a technical informational base, a psycho-social base and an ethical base. It is important to have the tools necessary to collect baseline data nationally, as presently a repository of this overall information does not exist."

Assistant Director of Nursing
Division of Maternal-Child Health
The Mount Sinai Medical Center
New York

II. DESCRIPTION OF PROBLEM SOLVING METHODOLOGY

Phase I

In the first 12 months, the project will

- survey and analyze current curriculums and teaching methodologies used in baccalaureate schools of nursing to prepare students for the beginning level practice of maternal-infant nursing.
- identify those schools which have implemented a range of competencies.
- develop a definition of competencies necessary for effective clinical and community-based beginning level practice for the extension of early and continuous prenatal care.

A panel of specialists – including clinical, public health, and curriculum experts and representatives from the American Nurses Association and National League for Nursing – will be convened to outline the full range of competencies, and make recommendations on the development of a survey tool to determine what is currently being taught and how.

The survey tool will be developed by project staff in collaboration with the co-directors and personnel of the three sponsoring organizations, and on the basis of the exchange of information with panel members and other practitioners in the maternal and child health field (Delphi Method). Inquiries to over 300 school of nursing will address teaching content and methodologies in the following major areas:

Maternal/Fetal Nursing
Neonatal Nursing
OB Clinical Experience
Supervision

The tabulation and analysis of responses to the questionnaire will contribute to a consensus at one or two subsequent meetings of the same panel of specialists on essential competencies, and how these might be incorporated in teaching programs. This will include consideration of the impact on the full curriculum for nursing education, the availability of faculty in specialized areas, and the impact on the hospital and community resources utilized in study programs.

The responses will identify those school which have successfully implemented a range of competencies, including mechanisms to measure and assure competencies in students, so that they can assist in the implementation of the competencies in other schools.

Phase II

The next 12 months will refine the competencies and develop a self-assessment tool for schools. These will proceed from requests for further information from schools that have incorporated a range of competencies, site visits to these schools, and another meeting of the panel.

Core competencies must take into account new scientific knowledge in the areas of human reproduction, obstetrics, neonatology, and parent-infant interactions. Maternity nurses must, for example, relate to diagnostic and treatment breakthroughs that have been achieved in relation to the "early confirmation of pregnancy, assessment of maternal and fetal well-being, detection of many diseases and defects in utero and, in certain situations, corrective measures that can be taken before the baby is born."[4]

On the community level, nurses must be able to counsel pregnant women and their families, identify high-risk cases in the early stages of pregnancy, and provide skilled ongoing prenatal care.

The core competencies that will be prepared for publication and incorporation in general nurse education programs will include descriptions of suggested didactic content, clinical experiences, and teaching/learning strategies.

On the basis of the preparation of a competencies model, the project will develop and publish a self-assessment tool for nursing schools to enable them to

- determine the competencies that need to be incorporated in study programs;
- evaluate faculty needs to implement new teaching components;
- review availability of clinical, technological and community learning resources to complement classroom instruction;
- measure their capacity to relate the needs of special population groups and adolescents to the instructional program;
- evaluate the impact of the incorporation of core competencies on general nurse training curriculums and on school budgets;
- determine their ability to develop mechanisms to assure competencies in students.

Phase III

This last phase (Year Three) will include the preparation of guidelines for the implementation of the competencies; the dissemination of information about the core competencies; the convening of regional meetings for review and discussion for the competencies; and the identification of sites for possible pilot testing of the program.

The implementation guidelines will describe how the teaching of perinatal nursing can be integrated in the full length of a general course of instruction, how didactic and clinical elements should be integrated, and how modern technologies can be incorporated in the study program.

The sponsoring organizations have the expertise, staff, and affiliations – with the further input of specialists and innovators at periodic panels and the regional meetings – to develop and evaluate project components, enlist the cooperation of schools of nursing, and obtain the input of health care practitioners in hospital and community services.

March of Dimes Birth Defects Foundation conducts a nationwide professional education program, summer workshops for nursing school faculty, and a broad public education program on maternal and infant health (See Appendix B). The American Association of Colleges of Nursin represents 357 university schools of nursing for the improvement of the practice of professional nursing through a) the advancement of the quality of baccalaureate and graduate programs in nursing, b) the promotion of research in nursing, and

c) the development of academic leadership (See Appendix C). The American College of Obstetricians and Gynecologists is the leading organization of professionals in the delivery of perinatal services. The Nurses' Association of the American College of Obstetricians and Gynecologists is the professional specialty organization for obstetric, gynecologic, and neonatal nurses, and seeks to promote the highest standards of OGN nursing practice, education and research (See Appendix D). Consultation with the American Nursing Association and the National League of Nurses is also planned.

The in-kind service of the three sponsoring organizations will include the supervision of March of Dimes' Vice President for Professional Education and the joint review and counsel of the administrative directors of AACN and NAACOG. They will oversee the development and implementation of all phases of the project; provide critical analysis; develop contacts with schools, agencies, and health care professionals; review evaluation plans and procedures; and advise schools of nursing on the adaptation of core competencies.

The March of Dimes will be responsible for project grant expenditures, fiscal reporting, budget review, and will provide facilities and data processing for the project office at its national headquarters.

III. DETERMINATION OF GOALS AND OBJECTIVES

The basic objectives of the grant are to:

1. Define the competencies necessary for beginning practitioners in maternal/infant health care, including the early and continuous care of those pregnant women and adolescents who customarily delay or avoid prenatal services. (First Year)
2. Identify and describe nursing school programs which have successfully implemented the competencies either wholly or partially, as a basis for the development of a variety of strategies to be used by other schools. (First Year)
3. Refine core competencies and develop a tool for nursing school self-assessment. (Second Year)
4. Disseminate information and have discussion of competencies in regional conferences. (Third Year)
5. Identify sites for pilot programs in schools which wish to upgrade their maternal/infant care curriculum. (Third Year)

Utilizing a panel of experts and then the Delphi Method, the views of faculty, community and hospital practitioners will be surveyed. The project will develop, assess and demonstrate a prototype of undergraduate study to meet the theoretical, clinical, regional and community-based requirements of maternal and infant care with emphasis on risk assessment and present underserved groups.

Didactic elements will include an overview of trends and issues in contemporary perinatology; the scientific bases for the assessment of the pregnant women, fetus and newborn; and concepts of care for women with high-risk pregnancies, adolescents, and neonates. The projected core competencies and implementation plan will underscore hands-on hospital and public health practice, including the development of skills in the handling of antenatal screening for the identification of risks; preventive care for childbearing women; labor monitoring and assessment; the monitoring of newborns at risk; and recognition of psychosocial-cultural aspects of maternal/infant health.

Designed to promote favorable pregnancy outcome, the core competencies framework will incorporate advances in science, expanded pharmaceutical knowledge, and a knowledge of the complications of pregnancy. On this basis, nurses will be able to relate more effectively to women in the prevention of maternal and infant disorders, and relate also to families in the identification of perinatal risks.

In summary, the goal of the project to be conducted by the three sponsoring organizations will be the preparation and demonstration of core competencies that will:

a. Develop beginning level skills for dealing with special population groups that pose high-risk problems in the public health field – i.e., adolescents and special cultural and ethnic populations – requiring the ability to relate to diverse individual, family and community situations.
b. Provide a theoretical and clinical basis for effective perinatal nursing, at the entry level, to enable the States to meet the service and technological demands particularly of high-risk maternal/fetal, maternal/newborn, and neonatal situations.
c. Develop a sound comprehension in the student nurse of the elements of assessment, planning, implementation and evaluation in primary perinatal care programs which utilize regionalized and community resources.

IV. PROJECT EVALUATION

The three phases of the project (12 months each) will be evaluated on the basis of the objectives set forth for each:

Phase I

Survey of maternal/infant health care content in curriculums of baccalaureate schools of nursing; development of definition of competencies necessary for early and continuous prenatal care. (First Year)

Information and data will be collected on the basis of a questionnaire survey of over 300 baccalaureate schools of nursing on their current course offerings and teaching methodologies. The questionnaire, to be reviewed by outside auditors, will list all the components of an optimum and comprehensive curriculum in the area of maternal/infant health care, and seek responses on what elements are presently being offered in the content of general nursing education.

The responses will be keypunched into the computer which will be programmed for data analysis on the basis of the following categories: Perinatology—trends and issues; Nursing process in family planning; Nursing process to improve the outcome of pregnancy; Prenatal care relating to physical, psychological and learning needs; High-risk pregnancy; Nursing care during stages of labor and delivery; Nursing care during puerperium; Assessment of mother postpartum; Nursing care of newborn; Complications occurring in the Newborn; Ethical, moral and legal problems; Perinatal health care teams; Follow-up.

The review of the survey responses will establish what fundamental components of maternal/infant health care are and are not presently being offered in undergraduate schools of nursing. This initial analysis will provide a basis for determination by the advisory panel and the co-sponsoring organizations on which core competencies may practicably be incorporated in general nursing education programs. The responses will also identify those schools that provide a range of competencies. Site visits to these schools will validate curriculum offerings as well as identify innovative teaching methodologies and clinical experiences.

Phase II

Refinement of maternal/infant health care competencies, and development of self-assessment tool for schools of nursing. (Second Year)

Outside consultants (panel) will evaluate recommended core competencies on the basis of the latest knowledge in maternal/infant health; imperatives in maternal/fetal/neonatal nursing; and the requirements of clinical and community-based nursing service for the delivery of early (first trimester) and continuous prenatal care.

The following basic criteria would be applied by the panel in the assessment of refined core competencies:

Perinatology – trends and issues

Health care services, regionalization, health manpower requirements, nursing roles and goals

Nursing process in family planning

Nursing care in infertility and contraception counseling

Nursing process to improve the outcome of pregnancy

Assessment, nursing diagnosis, intervention, teratologic factors, nutrition, preterm labor

Care during prenatal period relating to maternal, physical, psychological, and learning needs

High-risk pregnancy

Hemorrhagic complications, polyhydramnios, hyperemesis gravidarum, pre-clampsia, eclampsia, diabetes, cardiace disease, hypertension, infections, venereal disease, rubella

Nursing care during stages of labor and delivery

Coping ability, physical assessment, laboring pattern, evaluation of fetal response, administration of drugs and anesthesia, complications

Nursing care during puerperium

Assessment and intervention

Assessment of mother postpartum

Physical, emotional complications

Nursing care of newborn

Immediate evaluation, continuing observation, maintenance of adequate oxygenation, nutrition, positioning, maintaining body temperature, safety, comfort measures, sleep and rest, emotional needs of newborn and mother, transport

Complications occurring in the newborn

Respiratory, birth injuries, hemotylic disease infections, congenital anomalies, inborn errors of metabolism, chromosomal aberrations, preterm and low birth weight infants

Ethical, moral and legal problems of perinatal nursing care

Perinatal health care teams

Follow-up of high-risk mothers, infants and families

The same basic criteria will be applied in the evaluation of the self-assessment tool to be prepared for schools of nursing. In addition, the tool will be appraised from the standpoints of faculty needs, technological requirements, clinical and community-based study components, adaptability to general nursing education curriculums, the impact on school budgets, and applicability to mechanisms to test competencies in students.

Phase III

Preparation of guidelines for implementation of core competencies; regional meetings for dissemination and discussion of information and identification of potential sites for pilot testing of the program. (Third Year)

The discussion of the core competencies in the regional meetings will:

- assess their efficiency and cost effectiveness in the education of nurses for maternal/infant health care;
- provide a basis for critical analysis of innovative teaching methodologies before they are widely adopted;
- examine how special population groups and adolescents may be related to the teaching of core competencies despite current obstacles in the extension of perinatal services to these groups;
- develop recommendations on the interface of core competencies on the baccalaureate level with graduate and continuing education;
- obtain the reaction and perceptions of practitioners and nursing school faculty;
- assess the significance of the core competencies for the prevention of pre-term birth, the provision of information on nutritional requirements during pregnancy, and the modification of the behavior of pregnant women, including adolescents, from a variety of backgrounds and occupations;
- establish a basis for review of the potential of the core competencies for improving pregnancy outcomes;
- gauge the effectiveness of the core competencies in the training of nurses for the utilization of the technological and regional resources that presently exist in relation to maternal/infant health care;
- indicate what additional curricular and study materials are required.

V. ADAPTATION AND USE OF RESULTS

The project will provide to baccalaureate schools of nursing

- data and analysis on what is presently being taught in maternal/infant health care;
- core competencies for early and continuous prenatal care, including the care of the subgroup of women who have customarily delayed or avoided prenatal service;
- a tool for self-assessment;
- an implemental guide for schools of nursing for the development and testing of student competencies in maternal/infant health care.

On the basis of the in-kind input of the three sponsoring organizations, their various professional affiliations, and periodic panel and regional meetings, sites for a pilot program will be recommended.

The core competencies structure will meet substantially unmet needs in nursing education, and may subsequently influence standards for baccalaureate schools of nursing. It will impact on the quality of preventive and health promotion practices, and improve pregnancy outcome in general and special population groups. The latter – including various cultural minorities, the poor, adolescents, and working women at risk – represent a special challenge in the public health field.

PART III – BUDGET INFORMATION

SECTION A – BUDGET SUMMARY

Grant Program, Function or Activity (a)	Federal Catalog No. (b)	Estimated Unobligated Funds		New or Revieed Budget		
		Federal (c)	Non-Federal (d)	Federal (e)	Non-Federal (f)	Total (g)
1. Survey and Evaluation	13,232	$	$	$101,805	$	$101,805
2. Program Model & Self-Assess. Tool				127,645		127,645
3. Regional Meetings & Evaluation				123,543		123,543
4.						
5. Totals		$	$	$352,993	$	$352,993

SECTION B – BUDGET CATEGORIES

6. Object Class Categories	Grant Program, Function, or Activity				Total (5)
	Survey & Evaluation (1)	Model & Self Assess. Tool (2)	Regional Meetings & Evaluation (3)	(4)	
a. Personnel	$51,667	$56,833	$68,516	$	$177,016
b. Fringe Benefits	12,916	14,208	17,129		44,253
c. Travel (Site Visits)	1,333	16,667	2,667		20,667
d. Equipment					
e. Supplies	1,300	667	667		2,634
f. Contractual					
g. Construction					
h. Other (Tool Development, Survey, Meetings)	25,334	27,666	23,333		76,333
i. Total Direct Charges	92,550	116,041	112,312		320,903
j. Indirect Charges	9,255	11,604	11,231		32,090
k. TOTALS	$101,805	$127,645	$123,543	$	$352,993
7. Program Income	$	$	$	$	$

The adaptation of core competencies by schools of nursing will be in collaboration with federal and state maternal and child health offices concerned with development of nurses' capacity for the identification, assessment and monitoring of maternal/fetal risks, particularly in the first trimester; their understanding of the effects of disease and disability on newborns; and greater knowledge of procedures for early intervention and tracking in the care of these neonates. Non-classroom components in the model teaching program will incorporate new mechanisms for clinical and community-based learning

SECTION C – NON-FEDERAL RESOURCES

(a) Grant Program	(b) APPLICANT	(c) STATE	(d) OTHER SOURCES	(e) TOTALS
8.	$	$	$	$
9.				
10.				
11.				
12. TOTALS	$	$	$	$

SECTION D – FORECASTED CASH NEEDS

	Total for 1st Year	1st Quarter	2nd Quarter	3rd Quarter	4th Quarter
13. Federal	$101,805	$12,600	$32,600	$32,600	$24,005
14. Non-Federal					
15. TOTAL	$101,805	$12,600	$32,600	$32,600	$24,005

SECTION E – BUDGET ESTIMATES OF FEDERAL FUNDS NEEDED FOR BALANCE OF THE PROJECT

(a) Grant Program	FUTURE FUNDING PERIODS (YEARS)			
	(b) FIRST	(c) SECOND	(d) THIRD	(e) FOURTH
16. Program Model and Self-Assess. Tool	$127,645	$	$	$
17. Regional Meetings & Evaluation		123,543		
18.				
19.				
20. TOTALS	$127,645	123,543$	$	$

SECTION F – OTHER BUDGET INFORMATION

(Attach additional Sheets If Necessary)

21. Direct Charges: Start up, panel meetings, survey and evaluation, development of core competencies model and school self-assessment tool (to be published), planning and publicity for regional meetings, program evaluation.

22. Indirect Charges: 10%. Included are allocated costs for office space, telephones, utilities, and office equipment use including word processing, photocopy and computer.

23. Remarket: The March of Dimes' share of funding will constitute in-kind contributions by the Vice President for Professional Education, the staff of the Division of Professional Education, the Data Processing Department, and the Accounting Department. Non-budgeted in-kind contributions will also be made by the two co-sponsoring organizations: the American Association of Colleges of Nurses and the American College of Obstetricians and Gynecologists. The March of Dimes will underwrite the printing and distribution costs of all project publications.

PART IV PROGRAM NARRATIVE (Attach per instruction)

PHS-5161-1 (PAGE 9)

(Rev. 3 79)

experiences. New criteria will be established for learning skill evaluation by faculties to assure the competencies of students.

The adaptation of core competencies by schools of nursing will result in the development of new curricular materials, guidebooks and manuals as teaching aids in the education of nurses. These materials will emphasize, particularly, risk identification during the prenatal and infant periods.

We anticipate that on the basis of new core competency standards, study materials will be developed that will relate to theoretical content and clinical experience to such diverse perinatal topics as maternal nutrition, tertologic factors in pregnancy risks, the effects of various diseases on the mother/fetus/newborn, the significance of behavioral psychology and counseling during pregnancy particularly for adolescents and women from special cultural and socioeconomic groups, and the follow-up of high-risk mothers, infants and families.

Continuing education and graduate programs can utilize the core competencies. Continuing education can be the mechanism by which behaviors defined in the core competencies can be integrated in present practice. Once practitioners are competent, continuing education can define programs that will increase expertise in the area of maternal/infant health. Graduate programs will be able to use the competency statements to diagnose student learning needs, and design improved advanced curriculums.

NOTES

1. U.S. Department of Health and Human Service: Public Health Services, *Surgeon General's Workshop on Maternal and Infant Health,* Washington, D.C., 1981.

2. Fouts, J. and Fogel, C., "A Survey of Obstetrical Teaching Strategies in Baccalaureate School of Nursing," *Journal of Nursing Education*, Vol. 19, no. 7 (September, 1980), p. 26

3. Barnes, C.M., "Educational Preparation of Clinical Nurse Specialists for Children With Chronic Illness," (Paper prepared for Public Policies Affecting Chronically Ill Children and Their Families). Center for The Study of Families and Children, Institute for Public Policy Studies, Vanderbilt University, October 1982, pp. 18–19.

4. Mortimer B. Lipsett, M.D., "Achievements in Preventing Morbidity and Mortality by Researchers of the National Institute of Child Health and Human Development," *Public Health Reports,* Vol. 98, no. 1 (January-February, 1983), p. 47

Breinigsville, PA USA
31 May 2010
238934BV00001B/4/P